Disarmed: The Consequences of Gun Control in the West

John Shenton

Published by John Shenton, 2024.

DISARMED: THE CONSEQUENCES OF GUN CONTROL IN THE WEST

First edition. November 11, 2024.

Copyright © 2024 John Shenton.

ISBN: 979-8227524508

Written by John Shenton.

Also by John Shenton

Business Plan Basics
The Bahamas - More Islands and Recipes Than You Expect!
Collected Musings from Bricks and Mortar to E-commerce
The Smart City Odyssey: Unveiling the Secrets to Traveller-Centric
Software
The Dragon's Gambit: China's Bid for Global Dominance and the
Western Response
Silent Weapon
Business Basics: Money Sources
Influx
Fried Chips
Mandates, Motors, and Misinformation
Echos of Orwell
Control and Chaos
The Empire's Warning: What Rome's Fall Tells Us About the West
Today
Silent Slaves: The Dark Trade of Human Trafficking
Disarmed: The Consequences of Gun Control in the West

Table of Contents

Introduction

The debate surrounding gun control has become increasingly charged and polarised in recent years, especially within the Western world, where the right to self-defence clashes with concerns over public safety. As I examine this complex and multifaceted issue, my goal in this book is to untangle the strands of history, politics, and cultural values that have shaped contemporary gun policies in the USA, Europe, and the UK, highlighting the consequences both intended and unintended that these laws have wrought on society.

Gun control policies have long sought to protect citizens from gun violence. Yet, as violent crime surges, often fuelled by organised criminality, the conversation becomes ever more urgent. While many lawmakers believe restrictive gun laws are the answer, these policies have frequently led to paradoxical outcomes: instead of reducing violence, they sometimes embolden the criminal underworld, where traffickers and gangs can readily access firearms on the black market. Simultaneously, these same restrictions leave law-abiding citizens deprived of effective means for personal protection. My exploration will delve into this conundrum, examining the delicate balance between an individual's right to self-defence and society's need for safety.

Beginning with a historical overview, Chapter 1 provides context by tracing the philosophical and legal foundations of self-defence rights and how they evolved into the gun control policies we see today. The chapters that follow dissect the pressing realities of modern crime in Western societies where gun, drug, and human trafficking networks operate as an insidious triad, circumventing legal structures with ease. In this regard, I examine the extent to which open-border policies and mass migration have intensified these challenges, creating a breeding ground for organised crime and illegal arms trafficking. As I argue, a complex network has emerged, exploiting Western legal frameworks while endangering public safety.

In analysing these issues, I aim to address the wide-reaching effects of strict gun control on ordinary citizens. Chapters 2 through 6 lay out how these policies often leave responsible, law-abiding individuals exposed to dangers they cannot adequately guard against, from gang violence to black-market weapons. By focusing on specific case studies from American cities and European nations, I reveal how criminal networks circumvent laws, allowing dangerous weapons to proliferate even in countries with the strictest regulations. I explore how the defunding of police and shifting public safety policies compound these issues, stretching law enforcement's ability to combat illegal gun proliferation while inadvertently empowering those who operate outside the law.

One area deserving special attention is the psychological impact on citizens who feel defenceless in the face of rising crime. Chapter 9 tackles this sensitive subject, examining how the erosion of self-defence rights affects individual morale, alters social behaviours, and erodes public trust in governmental ability to provide security. When citizens are unable to protect themselves, fear becomes a dominant force, impacting not only daily life but also broader societal cohesion. To understand this, I draw on survey data, crime statistics, and first-hand accounts that reveal a growing anxiety about personal safety, particularly in areas where violent crime and gang activity are most pronounced.

In Chapters 7 through 10, I delve into comparative analyses of gun control policies in different regions, examining what has worked and what has not. By exploring the successes and failures of varying legal frameworks in the USA, Europe, and the UK, I highlight the complexities that arise when attempting to address gun violence through legislation alone. Countries with sweeping gun restrictions, such as the UK, often see high rates of unarmed violent crime, while regions in the USA with relaxed gun laws face distinct challenges. My analysis considers these examples with a critical eye, revealing how diverse cultural attitudes towards firearms influence policy effectiveness.

The final two chapters move towards solutions. Chapter 10 presents a critique of existing policies, noting areas where political short-sightedness and legislative overreach have exacerbated the problem, creating a divided society where the law-abiding public and the criminal underworld seem to inhabit parallel realities. Many of these policies ignore the criminal mechanisms that continue to thrive despite stringent laws, leaving the public vulnerable while failing to disrupt black-market weapon flows. I examine these issues through a balanced lens, incorporating expert perspectives and research to underline the disconnect between policy intentions and real-world outcomes.

In Chapter 11, I put forth a series of recommendations aimed at restoring equilibrium in gun policy. Here, my goal is to outline a practical, evidence-based approach that recognises the need for responsible self-defence while addressing the imperative to keep firearms out of criminal hands. This chapter advocates strengthening border controls, enhancing funding and resources for law enforcement, improving intelligence sharing across jurisdictions, and learning from successful models that have effectively balanced individual freedoms with public safety. It is, I believe, possible to craft policies that deter illegal gun access without stripping citizens of their right to protection. These recommendations aspire to help Western nations navigate the fine line between freedom and security, ensuring that measures taken to reduce violence do not come at the expense of personal rights.

In this exploration, I hope to provide not just an analysis of gun control and its consequences but a blueprint for a more balanced, effective approach to policy reform. Ultimately, governments have a duty to both protect their citizens and respect their freedoms.

4

Achieving this balance requires vigilance, pragmatism, and, above all, an unwavering commitment to policies rooted in reality, not ideology. I hope that this work will contribute to a more informed, rational conversation about gun policy, one that respects both the right to self-defence and the need for a secure, cohesive society.

Chapter 1: Introduction to Gun Control and Western Policy on Public Safety

The discourse around gun control in the West has long been characterised by heated debate, moral conviction, and deeply ingrained ideological rifts. At the heart of this issue lies a clash between the right to self-defence and the responsibility of the state to ensure public safety. In exploring this tension, we must first acknowledge the historical and philosophical frameworks that have shaped self-defence rights in Western societies, then examine how these principles have been challenged, reshaped, and, some would argue, dismantled by contemporary gun control policies.

From early English common law to the American founding documents, the right to defend oneself and one's family has traditionally been held as a sacrosanct principle in the West. This chapter begins by exploring the philosophical and legal underpinnings of self-defence in Western thought and then contrasts these with the more modern stance on gun control in the United States, Europe, and the United Kingdom. By unpacking the ideological evolution from self-defence as a personal right to the state as the primary arbiter of safety, I aim to provide a foundation for understanding the motivations behind these policies and assess their outcomes on societal safety.

Philosophical and Legal Foundations of Self-Defence Rights

The right to self-defence has deep roots in Western thought, perhaps most evidently seen in English common law. Centuries ago, self-defence was not merely a right but a duty to preserve one's life and autonomy. Thomas Hobbes, John Locke, and later thinkers posited that the right to life included the right to defend that life against harm. In Hobbes' social contract, self-defence was inalienable; a person's ultimate right was to protect themselves. For Locke, protecting "life, liberty, and property" was fundamental to civil society, with self-defence being the foundation of these rights. This concept evolved and crossed the Atlantic, underpinning the American Revolution and the subsequent crafting of the United States Constitution.

The American perspective on self-defence was uniquely codified in the Second Amendment, which explicitly enumerated the right to bear arms as a means of self-protection and a safeguard against tyranny. While this inclusion has been a point of enduring contention, particularly given the amendment's phrasing around the need for a "well-regulated militia," it unequivocally enshrined self-defence and resistance against oppression as fundamental rights. In contrast, the United Kingdom and European nations did not enshrine self-defence in the same explicit way, and over time, they moved toward a state-centred model of public safety.

The Shift Toward Gun Control

In the modern era, especially over the past century, gun control emerged as a reaction to social changes, with proponents arguing that reducing civilian access to firearms would mitigate violence and foster a safer society. Countries like the United Kingdom, many European nations, as well as Australia, New Zealand, and Canada have increasingly shifted the responsibility for safety onto the state, effectively eroding the long-held premise of self-defence as an individual right. This shift has been a steady, deliberate process, woven into evolving legal interpretations, public policies, and the expansion of state authority over personal liberties. What was once a fundamental expectation of each person's right and duty to defend themselves, their family, and property has now largely been recast as a collective responsibility, managed by the state and enforced through restrictive legislation. Many view this transformation as a recalibration of the citizen-state relationship, one that has diminished individual autonomy under the rationale of preserving public safety.

The erosion of self-defence as an individual right is perhaps nowhere more evident than in the sweeping bans and strict regulatory frameworks imposed on firearm ownership across these nations. Presented as essential measures to reduce criminal access to guns and prevent violence, these policies have led to significant consequences intended and otherwise. In the United Kingdom, the response to the 1996 Dunblane massacre saw a near-total ban on handguns, requiring those wishing to retain sporting or hunting rifles to navigate a complex and restrictive licensing process. Canada has enacted similar measures in recent years, with regulations now prohibiting specific semi-automatic firearms, high-capacity magazines, and, more recently, proposed "red flag" laws that allow law enforcement to seize firearms from individuals deemed dangerous. These measures, following mass shooting incidents in Nova Scotia and Quebec, were justified as critical steps toward reducing firearm-related violence.

Similarly, Australia implemented strict gun control legislation following the 1996 Port Arthur massacre, launching extensive buyback schemes and amnesties. New Zealand, after the Christchurch attack in 2019, followed suit by banning military-style semi-automatic firearms. Each of these policies has been framed as necessary for public safety, under the belief that disarming the public will reduce violence and foster a more peaceful society.

However, the results of these policies paint a complex and often troubling picture. While gun-related incidents did decline, especially mass shootings, other forms of violence and criminal activity have emerged as growing threats. In the United Kingdom, for instance, knife crime surged in urban centres like London, Manchester, and Birmingham after the handgun ban, showing that criminal elements simply adapted to other forms of weaponry rather than being discouraged by firearm restrictions. Australia, too, has seen rises in gang-related violence and organised crime, underscoring that gun control does little to affect the underground trafficking of arms. Canada's recent policies have not prevented criminal access to illegal guns, as most firearms used in gang activity are smuggled in from the

United States. This point highlights a key failure in these policies: while restrictions make it harder for law-abiding citizens to possess firearms, they do little to prevent criminal networks from accessing them through illegal channels.

In New Zealand, where a robust black market for firearms has developed following the recent bans, the disconnect between policy intentions and outcomes is striking. Just as with other countries, strict regulations do not erase the demand among criminals for firearms. They simply drive this demand underground, leading to the expansion of black-market operations that continue to supply guns to those who seek them. Canada's policies have faced challenges in curbing such illegal channels, especially with gang violence on the rise in cities like Toronto and Vancouver, where firearms smuggled across the border fuel an active black market.

These strict regulatory frameworks, however well-intentioned, overlook a critical reality: criminal elements are rarely discouraged by legal restrictions on firearms. Rather, they find ways to circumvent these laws, obtaining guns illegally or shifting to other methods of violence. In the meantime, law-abiding citizens, now deprived of their means to defend themselves, are left reliant on state protection that is increasingly stretched thin by funding constraints, resource limitations, and the complexities of rising crime rates. In each of these countries, the promise of safety has, in reality, left the average citizen more vulnerable and exposed to the unintended consequences of policies that may ultimately hinder their ability to protect themselves in an increasingly volatile world.

However, as we examine these policies, a few critical questions emerge: Has the removal of firearms from law-abiding citizens created safer societies? Or has it, perhaps counterintuitively, deprived individuals of the ability to defend themselves, leaving them more vulnerable in the face of escalating criminal activity? Consider the case of the United Kingdom, where restrictive gun laws were introduced in response to several high-profile violent incidents. In the wake of such tragedies, policymakers argued that disarming the public would curb violence. But in reality, violent crime, including knife attacks, surged in major cities following the 1997 ban on handguns. As this book will discuss in detail, such policies may achieve the opposite of their stated aims, fuelling a sense of insecurity among citizens who feel disempowered and unable to protect themselves.

Early Gun Control Policies and Their Intended Goals

Western countries that implemented gun control policies primarily did so intending to curb violence and protect citizens from mass attacks and crime. In the United States, policies targeting gun control began to emerge in the 20th century, motivated by rising urbanisation and concerns about gang violence. While some early measures were successful in targeting specific issues such as the infamous Tommy gun-wielding gangsters of Prohibition-era America these policies became increasingly broad, targeting not only criminals but the broader civilian population.

Europe, too, saw a wave of gun control legislation in the mid-to-late 20th century, with countries such as Germany, France, and Italy implementing policies aimed at reducing armed violence. In each instance, however, these policies carried unintended consequences. The focus on disarming the civilian populace often had the effect of creating unarmed, vulnerable segments of society while leaving criminals largely unimpeded in their access to black-market firearms. The initial aims of these policies to mitigate violence and protect citizens came into question as rising crime, drug trafficking, and human trafficking networks continued to exploit gaps in enforcement and porous borders.

In the United Kingdom, as previously mentioned, the sweeping bans following the Dunblane tragedy in 1996 were intended to prevent mass shootings and gun violence. Yet, violent crime rates in the UK, particularly knife crime, have steadily risen, suggesting that removing guns from law-abiding citizens did not diminish the tools or motivations of those determined to harm. For the average person, these policies have had a compounding effect, creating environments where they feel less safe and more reliant on a police force that is increasingly underfunded and overstretched.

Evaluating the Effectiveness of Gun Control in Promoting Public Safety

While gun control advocates cite specific instances of reduced firearm-related incidents, the broader trend is less conclusive. We see this vividly in areas where gun control laws are strictest, such as Chicago in the United States, where homicide rates have remained stubbornly high despite a near-total ban on firearms for civilians until recent legal changes. Similarly, parts of Europe that enacted sweeping gun control measures also continue to face high levels of organised crime and black-market arms trafficking.

The argument that disarming civilians promotes public safety becomes murkier when we factor in the rise of organised criminal networks, which continue to arm themselves through illegal means, making them effectively impervious to civilian disarmament. Meanwhile, the honest citizen, stripped of the means of self-defence, is left increasingly vulnerable. This vulnerability is further exacerbated by police underfunding and the pressures placed on law enforcement, which, even with the best intentions, cannot always respond swiftly enough to prevent harm.

Setting the Stage for the Emerging Consequences

As we continue to explore in this book, the consequences of gun control extend beyond simple statistics on crime or public safety. Rising criminal activity, increased drug trafficking, and human trafficking all operate within a space where law enforcement is often under-resourced, and citizens are unable to defend themselves. In examining these issues, I will argue that the net effect of restrictive gun policies has, in many cases, been to disempower the innocent, making law-abiding citizens more vulnerable to the very dangers gun control was meant to counter.

This chapter has sought to lay a foundation for understanding the ideological and historical bases of gun control in the West and why, despite good intentions, these policies often fail to deliver on their promises. In the chapters that follow, we will delve deeper into the unintended consequences of these policies, from the emboldenment of criminal elements to the expansion of trafficking networks, and what this all means for the everyday citizen caught in a cycle of dependency on state protection in an increasingly volatile world.

Chapter 2: The Impact of Mass Migration and Open Borders on Illegal Gun Trafficking

In recent years, the complex interplay between open-border policies, mass migration, and the rise of illegal gun trafficking has become increasingly apparent. As borders become more porous, driven by humanitarian crises and lax migration policies, illicit gun smuggling networks thrive, capitalising on unchecked flows of people and goods. This chapter delves into the correlation between these policies and the flourishing black market for firearms, focusing on the well-trodden smuggling routes from conflict zones into Western nations. Drawing from real-world case studies and statistical evidence, I will explore the mechanisms by which firearms make their way from regions of instability and violence to Western cities, where they contribute to a rise in organised crime and undermine public safety.

The Nexus of Mass Migration and Gun Trafficking: An Overview

The interrelation between mass migration and illegal gun trafficking is far from coincidental. Large-scale migration, especially from regions with significant political or economic turmoil, has strained Western border controls, creating opportunities for criminal syndicates. Desperate migrants often seek alternative pathways when traditional routes are unavailable or dangerous, and traffickers exploit these vulnerabilities. Gun runners and organised crime groups work together to disguise their operations within these migration flows, embedding firearms within legitimate-looking shipments or using human traffickers as intermediaries. In this context, weapons from areas plagued by war, poverty, and political instability find their way into the hands of criminals across Western cities, feeding the cycle of violence and jeopardising citizens' safety.

Open-border policies, while well-intentioned, have enabled this thriving underground network. They have reduced the efficacy of screening mechanisms, allowed traffickers to evade law enforcement, and increased the volume of migrants, making it challenging to discern between those seeking refuge and those smuggling illegal arms. Understanding this relationship is critical if we are to address the true scale of gun trafficking and develop strategies to protect citizens from the fallout of these policies.

Gun Smuggling Routes: From Conflict Zones to Western Streets

The routes by which illegal arms enter Western markets are varied, yet a few have proven consistently effective for traffickers. A notable route is the journey from the Southern Hemisphere through Latin America, directly into the United States across the US-Mexico border. Here, cartels and organised crime networks are deeply embedded within the fabric of the black market, thriving in areas where border enforcement is stretched thin or absent. Guns from Central and South American manufacturers, as well as surplus weapons from military and law enforcement entities, flow freely into the United States, making their way to crime-ridden urban areas, small towns, and even rural communities. This steady influx is exacerbated by local gangs, whose influence in trafficking firearms has grown, adding layers of complexity to an already deeply rooted problem.

The US-Mexico border is not alone in this predicament. The Mediterranean has also become a notorious corridor for illegal arms, with trafficking networks funnelling guns into Europe via maritime routes. Firearms originating in the Middle East and North Africa, where armed conflict is rife, often find their way into European markets through vulnerable coastal borders. Greece, Italy, and Spain frequently intercept arms shipments, yet countless others evade detection, arriving in Western Europe's major cities and arming criminal elements within those communities. In both cases, the movement of arms is bolstered by a permissive approach to migration, in which legitimate asylum seekers and traffickers alike traverse loosely controlled pathways.

The Role of Criminal Syndicates and Organised Crime

Organised crime syndicates are the prime beneficiaries of weakened borders. These groups, often highly structured and globally connected, view mass migration as an ideal cover for their gun trafficking operations. They capitalise on the ambiguity of migrant flows, embedding weapons into caravans or consignments that are otherwise assumed to contain household goods or agricultural produce. By exploiting weak points in border enforcement, criminal organisations can readily slip firearms past inspections.

The connection between arms trafficking and migration is particularly stark in the US, where Mexican drug cartels dominate gun-smuggling routes. These groups maintain extensive networks within both the US and Mexico, facilitating the movement of firearms alongside their primary narcotics trade. With US authorities focusing much of their attention on the drug trade, guns are often overlooked or hidden within the larger stream of illegal goods. Similarly, in Europe, Mediterranean routes are frequented by North African gangs that smuggle arms alongside human cargo, using both regular and irregular migration channels to move weapons from point of origin to market.

A striking example of this trend can be found in the recent rise of so-called "ghost guns" – firearms that are manufactured in parts and assembled covertly, leaving no serial numbers or tracking marks. Organised crime has swiftly adopted this technology, purchasing parts and distributing them along smuggling routes, exploiting porous borders to evade regulation. These weapons are particularly problematic, as they undermine Western law enforcement efforts to control gun violence by making it nearly impossible to trace guns used in crimes back to their source.

Porous Borders and Vulnerability of Western Citizens

One of the most concerning aspects of this complex issue is the impact on ordinary citizens. While policies increasingly focus on strict gun control for law-abiding citizens, comparatively less attention is directed toward the spread of illegal firearms in criminal networks. This imbalance raises questions: why are legal gun owners more closely scrutinised while black-market operations continue to flourish? Open-border policies, though rooted in humanitarian ideals, unintentionally provide opportunities for firearms trafficking that ultimately increase risks for local populations. Criminal groups exploit these routes, bringing firearms into urban centres already strained by socioeconomic challenges and limited police presence.

The influx of unregulated arms into Western societies has empowered criminal factions, particularly in urban areas. As guns circulate freely on the black market, they fuel a surge in gang violence, armed robberies, and drug-related shootings. Tragically, these violent incidents tend to disproportionately affect low-income communities, where residents already face challenges like under-resourced law enforcement and prolonged response times. Despite evidence that criminal misuse of firearms drives much of the violence, efforts remain concentrated on curbing access for legal owners.

This focus raises fundamental questions about the allocation of resources and priorities. Implementing stringent gun control measures for law-abiding individuals without addressing the root causes of illegal firearms trafficking leaves society vulnerable to escalating violence. The paradox lies in the fact that criminals by definition ignore gun laws, leaving communities defenceless and crime-ridden, while lawful citizens bear the brunt of restrictive policies. Rebalancing enforcement strategies to prioritise dismantling trafficking networks over tightening lawful gun ownership could help mitigate these risks without compromising responsible gun rights.

To address this, it's crucial to deploy a targeted approach focusing on cross-border intelligence and cooperative international policing to track and halt illegal firearms entering the country. Robust enforcement at known trafficking points and fortified collaborations between domestic and international agencies could greatly reduce the flow of illegal firearms. This recalibration would not only protect citizens but also honour the principles of balanced and fair public safety, ensuring that lawful gun ownership is respected even as illegal trafficking is forcefully curtailed.

There is also the psychological toll of knowing that criminal groups have become emboldened by a lack of border enforcement. Communities feel the strain of unchecked gun trafficking as the influx of illegal firearms permeates daily life. In cities like London, Paris, and Los Angeles, formerly isolated incidents of gun violence have become alarmingly common, particularly in neighbourhoods populated by recent migrants. This increase in armed violence has eroded public trust, not only in law enforcement but also in government institutions perceived as prioritising open-border policies over the security of their citizens.

Case Studies: US-Mexico Border Crossings, U.K. and Mediterranean Routes

Examining specific cases brings the harsh reality of this issue into sharp focus. The gun trafficking dynamics along the U.S.-Mexico border underscore a complex, two-way flow that intensifies violence and fortifies cartel power. An estimated 200,000 firearms are illegally trafficked across this border annually, with many weapons originating in the U.S. before being smuggled into Mexico. Cartels favour these arms, especially high-powered rifles like AK-47s and AR-15s, which are trafficked through porous areas such as Texas, Arizona, and California, where limited oversight on private gun sales and "straw purchases" (when someone buys a gun legally on behalf of another) fuels their trade. This has led to powerful, well-armed criminal organisations that operate with force against law enforcement, government officials, and civilians alike.

Once firearms reach the cartel networks, their impact is immediate and deadly. The cartels employ these weapons not only for territorial control but also to protect their smuggling routes for drugs and human trafficking operations into the United States. Weapons from the U.S. significantly enhance the firepower of Mexican cartels, placing them in frequent, violent clashes with law enforcement, resulting in high casualties and undermining any attempts at regional stability. Each weapon smuggled southward intensifies a spiral of violence that affects communities in both countries.

On the U.S. side, border control is similarly compromised by the presence of these trafficked firearms, as cartel affiliates and gangs smuggle guns and drugs into American cities. The vicious cycle created here makes any singular effort ineffective: while U.S. agencies may target trafficking rings, the demand for high-calibre firearms and the proximity to suppliers ensure that cartels are rarely short on supply. This cycle makes cross-border cooperation essential yet challenging, given the vast, often sparsely monitored stretches of borderland.

Moreover, the pattern of trafficking reveals sophisticated networks capable of avoiding detection, often exploiting both legal loopholes and corrupt officials on both sides of the border. Weapons travel through specific "trafficking corridors" with origins in states like Texas, where relaxed gun laws enable easier purchases. These guns are then disassembled and hidden in compartments within vehicles or concealed among goods, complicating border inspection efforts. Cartels often deploy scouts and lookouts to monitor enforcement efforts along these corridors, making their smuggling operations highly adaptive.

The profits from this illicit trade enable cartels to diversify their operations, further consolidating their influence over territories in Mexico and even in the U.S. The challenge posed by this arms influx is not only one of law enforcement but also of policy; a holistic response to border security, gun control, and cartel disruption is essential to reduce the flow of arms southward and break the cycle of violence along the border.

Addressing the issue requires recognising it as a transnational problem involving crime networks, regulatory gaps, and regional socio-political consequences that go beyond either of the country's jurisdictions.

The UK has become increasingly susceptible to gun smuggling as organised crime groups seek new avenues to introduce illicit firearms. Case studies highlight several routes and methods utilised by traffickers, including exploiting shipping containers, hidden compartments in vehicles, and even postal services to transport weapons undetected. For instance, firearms sourced from Eastern Europe, particularly from former Yugoslavian nations with a surplus of military-grade weaponry, are often smuggled into the UK through lorry and ferry routes across the English Channel. One such operation, uncovered by the National Crime Agency (NCA), involved a lorry intercepted in Dover carrying a cache of handguns hidden within household items, demonstrating the cunning methods employed by traffickers.

Another significant case involved parcels mailed from the United States, which has been a known source of firearms smuggled into the UK due to the sheer number of illegal guns available in the USA. These shipments, often marked as innocuous items, bypass initial scrutiny, leveraging the sheer volume of daily mail to avoid detection. In 2015, the NCA thwarted a network importing pistols and revolvers through mail services, exposing how traffickers exploit both cross-border trade and vulnerabilities in the postal system.

Moreover, the internet and dark web marketplaces have opened new channels for arms procurement, allowing traffickers to coordinate purchases anonymously and evade traditional law enforcement surveillance. In one case, law enforcement discovered that criminals had been purchasing gun components online and assembling them once they arrived in the UK, circumventing more direct detection methods.

These cases reveal a troubling adaptability among smugglers, who continually refine their tactics in response to strengthened border controls. The challenge for UK law enforcement, then, lies in staying ahead of these evolving techniques, requiring sophisticated intelligence operations and international cooperation to prevent firearms from reaching criminal networks across the nation.

Italy's challenges with arms smuggling through Mediterranean migration routes illustrate a troubling reality: the same pathways intended for asylum and humanitarian entry have become conduits for illicit arms. Amid waves of economic migrants and asylum seekers, traffickers exploit these established routes, embedding firearms, ammunition, and explosives within migrant shipments bound for Europe. Italian authorities have intercepted boats loaded not only with migrants but with hidden caches of weaponry, some originating from conflict zones in Libya and Syria, and destined for distribution across Europe.

This dynamic is exacerbated by the near impossibility of thoroughly inspecting every vessel arriving from areas rife with conflict. Often departing from Libya's destabilised shores, these boats represent both human desperation and sophisticated smuggling operations. Traffickers skillfully leverage the humanitarian response frameworks, circumventing scrutiny by mingling arms within otherwise legitimate-looking shipments. Such shipments bring significant security concerns, as organised crime groups and potential terrorist actors gain access to weaponry previously isolated to conflict regions.

For Italy and its European neighbours, the Mediterranean has effectively transformed into an unregulated frontier for illicit goods. Italian ports have reported an increase in seizures of arms along these routes, highlighting both the ingenuity and adaptability of traffickers. Their operations expose not only the logistical challenges that arise in monitoring vast, open waters but also the unintended consequences of porous borders. As Italy and other EU nations grapple with this evolving threat, the need for cooperative border management and intelligence-sharing becomes ever more urgent.

In essence, Mediterranean arms trafficking illustrates how humanitarian and security concerns can collide, creating a scenario where unchecked migration flows unwittingly bolster criminal networks with access to arms intended for violent and destabilising purposes. Addressing this will require a reassessment of border protocols, balancing the humanitarian imperative with the pressing security needs posed by organised smuggling operations.

These cases underscore the necessity of stricter border enforcement policies. Without the ability to discern between legitimate migrants and traffickers, border agencies remain unable to stem the flow of arms effectively. While humanitarian concerns are valid and urgent, the reality is that unchecked migration has exacerbated Western nations' vulnerability to gun violence, creating fertile ground for trafficking networks.

Balancing Security and Humanitarian Needs

The correlation between mass migration, open borders, and illegal gun trafficking is undeniable. Open-border policies, though often rooted in noble humanitarian principles, have unintentionally provided fertile ground for criminal enterprises to flourish, jeopardising the safety of law-abiding citizens. Criminal syndicates have proven adept at leveraging weaknesses in border enforcement, embedding firearms within migration flows to bypass regulations and expand their market reach.

To achieve both security and compassion, we must implement effective, targeted border control measures without compromising humanitarian principles. Yet, as policymakers increase restrictions on lawful gun ownership, it appears the same rigour is lacking in tackling the illegal arms smuggling that empowers criminal networks. Current policy often impacts law-abiding citizens while criminal syndicates exploit gaps in border oversight, profiting from the absence of robust enforcement measures.

Enhanced intelligence-sharing, collaborative inspections and fortified partnerships between immigration and law enforcement agencies could bridge this gap. Such steps would provide a crucial framework to intercept illicit firearms trafficking, effectively disrupting the criminal networks operating across borders. Tighter coordination could enable better surveillance and inspection without hindering legitimate asylum processes, and targeted operations along well-documented trafficking routes would mitigate the criminal misuse of firearms while minimising the impact on innocent migrants.

The focus must shift from increasing restrictions on those who adhere to legal firearm ownership to targeting the criminal operations undermining our safety. Addressing this dual priority of protecting citizens from illegal arms while preserving humanitarian commitments requires pragmatism and resolve. If not, we risk leaving citizens vulnerable to violent crime while burdening those who follow the law with excessive limitations. The challenge, therefore, is to balance compassionate policies with stringent security measures, ensuring that the arms reaching our communities come only through lawful channels and that criminal misuse, not lawful ownership, becomes the primary focus of enforcement.

Chapter 3: Legal Restrictions on Firearms Ownership and the Burden on Law-Abiding Citizens

As I delve into this chapter, I find myself compelled to address a poignant reality: while governments across the Western world enforce ever-tightening restrictions on firearms, these regulations often place the heaviest burden on those who adhere to the law the very citizens these laws claim to protect. The fundamental principle of self-defence, deeply embedded in Western philosophical and legal traditions, is increasingly compromised by restrictive gun policies. These policies, intended to reduce violence, often miss their target, leaving citizens defenceless and tipping the balance in favour of those who operate outside the law.

Throughout this chapter, I will examine how firearm restrictions disproportionally affect law-abiding citizens, failing to prevent criminals from accessing guns while stripping ordinary people of essential self-defence options. By reviewing case studies from various countries, such as the UK and the USA, I'll illustrate how restrictive gun policies fall short of their objectives and expose the growing disparity between criminals and citizens in terms of personal security.

The Irony of Gun Control: A Deterrent for the Law-Abiding, Not for Criminals

In the UK, where firearms laws are among the strictest in the world, law-abiding citizens face almost insurmountable barriers to gun ownership. Legislation such as the Firearms Act of 1968 and the subsequent amendments have made legal ownership of most firearms prohibitively difficult. These regulations, although arguably well-intentioned, effectively treat responsible, law-abiding citizens with the same suspicion as hardened criminals. This oversight burdens citizens with extensive background checks, long waiting periods, and arduous licencing requirements while criminals, unburdened by such legal encumbrances, continue to access firearms through illicit means.

Case studies reveal a troubling pattern that echoes through neighbourhoods and cities across the UK: stringent laws have not succeeded in curbing violent crime. In stark contrast to the intended goals of these restrictions, knife attacks and shootings persist with alarming regularity, challenging the effectiveness of such policies. The underlying assumption that by tightly controlling legal firearm ownership, the state can create a safer society appears increasingly flawed. Official statistics only underscore this grim reality. In 2019, the Metropolitan Police reported a 26 per cent increase in knife crime and a notable rise in gun-related violence, with London bearing the brunt of these crimes.

In many firearm-related crimes in the UK, identifying the exact weapon used can be challenging unless reported by witnesses, identified through forensics, or recovered with the suspect. For instance, during the year ending in September 2022, a total of 6,369 firearm offences were reported, of which 2,245 involved imitation firearms such as replicas, BB guns, and blank-firing guns. Real handguns accounted for a substantial portion, with 1,990 instances due to their concealability and ease of trafficking.

Offences involving firearms most commonly involved violence against persons, with 2,267 cases reported. Other notable cases included robberies (941), burglaries (160), and public threats or intimidation (293), highlighting firearms' frequent use in threats, intimidation, and criminal activities. Knife crime, however, remains significantly more prevalent, particularly in armed robberies, with 16,994 cases recorded compared to 797 involving firearms over a similar period. The presence of firearms in homicides in 31 cases in the same year, including two police officers remains far below knife-related homicides, which numbered 282.

Yet, despite these numbers, firearm-related crime is on an upward trajectory, evidenced by 1,151 possession offences alone in the same timeframe. The steady rise in possession and firearm offences reflects ongoing issues with illegal weapon trafficking and usage, challenging the assumption that stringent legal restrictions effectively reduce such criminal activities.

Despite the intention to remove weapons from the hands of dangerous individuals, restrictive gun laws have seemingly only created a safe environment for those willing to disregard the law entirely.

For many, the situation is nothing short of a paradox. Firearms are theoretically "controlled," with rigorous restrictions preventing citizens from legally purchasing guns for personal protection. Yet, in practice, the black-market supplies firearms to violent criminals with relative ease. Organised crime syndicates and illicit arms traffickers continue to exploit weak points in international supply chains, bringing a steady flow of illegal firearms into the country. These weapons, readily available to those who seek them out, enable criminals to operate with a sense of impunity, while law-abiding citizens face significant obstacles in attempting to protect themselves. Far from deterring violent crime, these laws create a situation in which only those outside the law are armed, while law-abiding citizens are left virtually defenceless.

The impact of this disparity is deeply felt in the lives of ordinary people. For the average citizen in the UK, options for self-defence are extraordinarily limited. Legal access to a firearm for home defence is practically impossible under current legislation, and even non-lethal alternatives such as pepper spray, Tasers, or batons are categorised as offensive weapons. Simply possessing these items can lead to criminal charges, regardless of the context in which they might be used. This restrictive approach effectively removes any viable self-defence options, making individuals reliant on police intervention in situations where immediate action is often needed but rarely available in time.

The tragic irony here is glaring: those most committed to following the law, who would use defensive tools only as a last resort, are rendered vulnerable, left to hope that assistance arrives swiftly enough in the face of an attack. They bear the brunt of these restrictions, effectively disarmed and dependent on the state for protection that is frequently out of reach. The current system is thus stacked against law-abiding citizens, who must navigate the reality of rising violence while remaining without the means to defend themselves effectively. Meanwhile, criminals, who have little regard for gun control laws, remain well-armed and emboldened by a system that ultimately benefits them. This duality a society in which criminals can arm themselves freely while law-abiding citizens are strictly controlled poses serious questions about the role of government in ensuring the safety and autonomy of its people.

This disparity has fostered an unsettling environment where trust in law enforcement and government policy is eroding. Citizens increasingly feel they are treated as potential threats by the state simply for seeking the right to protect themselves, while criminals exploit the limitations of an overstretched police force. For instance, the UK's limited police resources are strained by the demands of addressing rising crime rates, leaving many people in high-crime areas vulnerable, with long response times exacerbating the problem. In essence, the restrictive gun policies fail not only in their stated aim of reducing violence but also in safeguarding the rights and security of law-abiding citizens.

In examining this scenario, one must ask: what is the ultimate aim of these policies? Are they truly designed to protect citizens, or do they serve as a means of control over the populace, stifling any possibility of self-defence in a manner that seems disproportionately restrictive? By leaving citizens without viable self-defence options, the state places a substantial burden on its ability to deliver safety, all the while placing law-abiding citizens at greater risk. The tragic irony is that, in seeking to protect the public through stringent firearm laws, the government has inadvertently shifted the balance of power towards criminals those least likely to respect the law and most likely to exploit its weaknesses.

This scenario is not unique to the UK. In cities across the United States, restrictive firearm policies, particularly in areas like Chicago, New York, and Los Angeles, have left ordinary citizens defenceless while failing to reduce gun-related violence significantly. Chicago, for instance, enforces some of the strictest gun control laws in the country, yet suffers from one of the highest rates of gun violence. It raises an uncomfortable question: if gun control policies effectively reduce violence, why do these heavily regulated cities face endemic gun crime? Evidence suggests that such policies are, at best, ineffective and, at worst, exacerbate the very issues they purport to solve.

Case Studies of Defenceless Citizens in the Face of Criminal Violence

There are numerous instances where restrictive gun policies have left citizens defenceless, often with devastating consequences. In one particularly heart-wrenching case in the UK, a woman named Sarah was stalked by an ex-partner who repeatedly violated restraining orders. Despite clear evidence of imminent danger, Sarah was legally barred from carrying any form of self-defence. One evening, her stalker broke into her home and attacked her before the police could intervene. Sarah's case underscores a painful truth: legal barriers prevented her from possessing the means to defend herself, leaving her at the mercy of her assailant. This tragic reality raises profound ethical questions about the right to self-defence and the state's responsibility for failing to secure that right for its citizens.

In the United States, similar cases have occurred where individuals living in high-crime areas are prevented from arming themselves due to local gun laws. Consider the story of an elderly man in New York who was targeted by a repeat offender. Living in a city with stringent gun control laws, he faced significant barriers to legal gun ownership. His vulnerability, created by legal restrictions, emboldened the criminal, who viewed him as an easy target. Such cases illustrate that rather than reducing crime, restrictive gun policies often embolden criminals by stripping law-abiding citizens of their defensive capabilities.

Comparative Analysis: The UK and the USA

In comparing the UK's experience with that of the USA, we observe striking similarities and differences that shed light on the efficacy or lack thereof of restrictive gun policies. The UK has embraced near-total civilian disarmament, relying on a comprehensive legal framework that bans most firearms and limits access to less-lethal defensive tools. Yet, the nation's violent crime rates particularly knife and firearm assaults are climbing. Citizens in cities like London and Manchester, where knife violence is particularly acute, have little to protect themselves against armed assailants. Although the UK government enforces policies that penalise even minor infractions related to self-defence, criminal networks continue to thrive, and violent crime persists.

In the United States, the varying outcomes of restrictive versus permissive gun policies expose crucial insights into the relationship between citizen empowerment and crime deterrence. Chicago, a city with some of the strictest gun regulations in the country, serves as a striking example where stringent laws on firearm ownership have not curbed the prevalence of gun violence. Here, despite robust regulations intended to reduce firearm accessibility, illegal weapons remain readily available, saturating the streets and fuelling an unrelenting cycle of violence. This paradox has raised uncomfortable questions about the effectiveness of disarming law-abiding citizens, especially when they find themselves at the mercy of criminals who have no qualms about breaking these same laws.

On the other hand, states with more relaxed gun ownership policies, such as Texas, offer a contrasting model. In Texas, firearm ownership is both widespread and accessible, and yet, interestingly, violent crime rates do not match those of high-crime urban areas with stringent restrictions. While Texas is not without its share of crime, the lower levels of violent gun-related incidents in many areas suggest that a population empowered with the means for self-defence could indeed play a role in deterring criminal activity. The rationale here is grounded in the deterrent effect: the mere knowledge that potential victims might be armed could dissuade would-be offenders.

This disparity between Chicago and Texas highlights a broader issue: restrictive policies tend to impact law-abiding citizens more severely than the criminals they aim to target. In cities like Chicago, those who wish to adhere to the law and responsibly arm themselves for protection face substantial bureaucratic and legal hurdles. Meanwhile, criminal elements sidestep these restrictions entirely, benefitting from illicit firearm networks that operate with remarkable impunity. The result is a glaring gap in personal security, with responsible citizens left vulnerable and defenceless while criminals remain well-armed and emboldened.

Examining the impact of such policies through the lens of citizen empowerment versus government control brings into question the ultimate purpose of these restrictive measures. While their intent may be to foster public safety, their outcomes often suggest an unbalanced approach that fails to address the real root of gun violence illegally trafficked firearms and organised crime. Instead of primarily focusing on illegal supply chains and improving law enforcement's ability to dismantle these operations, restrictive policies tend to be designed around the notion that fewer legal firearms in circulation will lead to a safer society. The experiences of various U.S. states reveal a more complex picture, one that suggests that lawful gun ownership might serve as a counterbalance to unchecked criminal activity.

There is a sense of empowerment that accompanies the right to self-defence a principle that is deeply rooted in the American ethos and law. i.e., *The "Second Amendment of the US Constitution—Bearing Arms"*

A well-regulated Militia, being necessary to the security of a free State, the right of the people to keep and bear Arms shall not be infringed.

Yet restrictive gun policies risk undermining this by inadvertently creating environments where law-abiding citizens are rendered powerless against well-armed criminals. The disparity between the legally disarmed and the illegally armed has only grown starker, highlighting the limitations of an approach that fails to distinguish between responsible ownership and criminal intent. As we consider the broader implications of these policies, it becomes increasingly clear that genuine safety may lie not in disarming the public but in empowering citizens while targeting the sources of illegal firearms with greater precision and resolve.

Government Regulations and the Reality They Overlook

A significant problem with restrictive firearm policies is that they often overlook the realities of criminal behaviour. Criminals, by nature, operate outside the law; therefore, legal constraints around firearm access do not apply to them in practice. In places like the UK and certain American cities, black markets provide a steady supply of illegal firearms, easily bypassing official regulations. Moreover, these markets are bolstered by organised crime networks that thrive on the demand created by unarmed, defenceless populations.

The assumptions underpinning restrictive gun policies are flawed in several respects. Policymakers often assume that reducing the number of legal firearms correlates with reduced violence, an assumption belied by rising crime rates in gun-free zones. Rather than acknowledging the failure of these policies, governments often double down, further restricting gun ownership while ignoring the proliferation of illegal weapons. This disconnect between policy intent and on-the-ground realities leads to regulations that, while severe, are ineffective in achieving their stated goal: enhancing public safety.

The Unintended Consequences of Gun Control

When I examine the consequences of restrictive gun policies, it becomes apparent that these regulations often have unintended effects that exacerbate the issues they aim to resolve. By limiting self-defence options, governments inadvertently create environments where criminals hold a substantial advantage over ordinary citizens. This dynamic undermines not only public safety but also the citizen's sense of security and autonomy. Furthermore, in rendering citizens dependent on state intervention for protection, restrictive gun policies fuel a cycle of helplessness, leaving individuals reliant on overstretched and underfunded law enforcement agencies.

Consider also the psychological impact of living in a society where self-defence is discouraged or outright forbidden. Many people report feeling powerless and vulnerable, particularly in areas plagued by gang violence or drug-related crime. In communities where police response times are long and law enforcement resources are strained, residents find themselves with limited recourse. This imbalance between criminals and ordinary citizens corrodes trust in the state's ability to protect its people and calls into question the legitimacy of policies that sacrifice individual safety for an illusory sense of control over firearms.

Re-evaluating Firearm Restrictions for Public Safety

It is therefore crucial to re-evaluate firearm restrictions through the lens of practical outcomes rather than ideological objectives. The evidence suggests that restrictive policies may offer symbolic reassurance but do little to protect citizens from the harsh realities of criminal violence. The most troubling aspect of these policies is their disproportional impact on law-abiding citizens, leaving them defenceless while failing to curb criminal access to firearms. If the purpose of gun control is to promote public safety, then it must be held accountable for achieving that end, rather than merely penalising those who abide by the law.

As I look ahead to the subsequent chapters, the issues raised here will continue to surface as mass migration and open borders further complicate gun control efforts, bringing new challenges as illegal firearms cross borders with relative ease. The pressing need for a balanced, evidence-based approach to gun policy, one that respects both public safety and individual rights, has never been more evident. The question remains: will governments have the courage to confront the true drivers of violent crime, or will they persist in disarming those who are most vulnerable?

Chapter 4: Guns, Drugs, and Organised Crime: The Triad of Modern Criminality

The interlocking worlds of illegal firearms, drug trafficking, and organised crime represent an unyielding triad that has increasingly come to define modern criminality in both the West and beyond. Each element is both catalyst and consequence, feeding off and reinforcing the others in a cycle of violence and destabilisation that has taken root within our communities. In this chapter, I will delve into the intricate web that binds these criminal enterprises, illustrating how the narcotics trade, fuelled by unrelenting demand and high-profit margins, relies on the availability of firearms to enforce its territorial dominance, protect its operations, and deter both rivals and law enforcement alike.

Organised crime networks, ever adaptive, have capitalised on the prohibition and restriction of these commodities, creating highly lucrative black markets where drugs, guns, and power are traded and wielded with deadly efficiency. This symbiotic relationship, in which the presence of one component invariably bolsters the need for the others, has become a defining feature of the modern criminal underworld. Throughout this chapter, I shall use case studies and examples from regions where this convergence is most pronounced: from cartel-influenced communities in the USA to European cities grappling with the spillover effects of gang-related violence. I will also examine how well-intentioned but ineffective gun control policies have left ordinary citizens increasingly vulnerable, and restricted from protecting themselves while the power and reach of organised crime remains largely unmitigated.

The Nexus of Narcotics and Firearms

To understand the pervasive grip of organised crime, one must first comprehend the interplay between the narcotics trade and illegal firearms. Narcotics markets are not sustained merely by the availability of drugs but by the underlying power structures that allow these markets to operate unchallenged. In the USA, particularly along the southern border, the convergence of narcotics and firearms forms a toxic nexus that fuels violence on a massive scale. The situation, once largely contained to Mexico, has grown far beyond the border, deepening its impact on American cities and towns. This interdependent network where guns fuel the drug trade and drugs fund the arms supply has established a powerful foothold, with both cartel violence and organised crime networks now entrenched within the United States. This cycle is facilitated by the flow of narcotics from South and Central America, crossing into the USA and dispersed by a complex, sprawling web of traffickers who work in tandem with gang networks. These traffickers and gangs bring with them the modus operandi that has enabled Mexican cartels to control vast swathes of territory in their homeland, effectively exporting a model of violent enforcement and territorial dominance that is now plaguing U.S. communities.

The role of firearms within this structure is both alarming and illuminating. Firearms, for these organisations, are not simply tools of intimidation or violence they are the backbone of their operational strategy. The cartels and affiliated gangs use firearms to establish their dominance, ruthlessly enforcing their territorial control with a mix of calculated intimidation and open violence. High-calibre assault rifles, handguns, and semi-automatic weapons are smuggled alongside narcotics, their presence a testament to the cartel's power. Here, one sees firearms not merely as weapons but as instruments of governance; for these groups, wielding power over a neighbourhood or city block means wielding firepower.

This reality has only been exacerbated by policies that allow for porous borders and inadequate checks, particularly under the Democratic Party's open-border approach in recent years. These policies have created unintended consequences, as the laxity in enforcement provides criminal organisations with the permeability they need to expand their operations seamlessly into American territory. The reach of the cartels is no longer limited to distant, rural areas along the border; it has infiltrated cities and suburbs alike. Law enforcement agencies across states, from California to Texas, increasingly report cartel-linked gang activity in urban centres, where these networks align themselves with local gangs, creating a synergistic relationship that benefits both sides. Through this alignment, the cartels bring a structured hierarchy and an enforcement model honed by decades of violent experience, while local gangs offer an intimate knowledge of the American urban landscape, facilitating an entrenched cycle of violence, trafficking, and intimidation.

The effect of this expansion is profound and deeply unsettling. In many cases, these cartels and their American gang affiliates operate as though they are above the law, capable of exerting a kind of shadow governance in the areas they dominate. This dominance is perpetuated by firearms, which function as both tools and symbols of power. Cartels rely on armed enforcers who deploy brutal violence to maintain order and loyalty within their ranks, ensuring that no one dares to question their authority. Those within the hierarchy of these organisations are expected to follow orders without question, with loyalty maintained not through trust or allegiance but through fear a fear imposed and reinforced by the omnipresent threat of gun violence.

This new era of cartel influence, now no longer limited to border towns but embedded within the heart of American cities, reveals a dark irony in the context of American gun control policies. While state and federal regulations attempt to limit firearm access for civilians, they do little to deter cartels, whose international operations and complex smuggling networks render such laws moot. For the average citizen, these restrictions represent a curtailing of their right to self-defence, especially in communities increasingly affected by cartel-related violence. The reality is that these restrictions do not address the guns in the hands of criminals; instead, they often limit the defensive options available to law-abiding citizens, who are then left in the crossfire of a battle waged by forces entirely unrestrained by these laws.

Thus, firearms are woven into the very fabric of cartel operations, signifying both how these groups maintain control and the stark reality that criminal networks, once confined to Mexico, have evolved into multinational enterprises. These enterprises are driven not only by profit but by a ferocious need for dominance that transcends national borders, sustained by the relentless trafficking of drugs and arms. Without addressing the fundamental issues that enable these networks to thrive the porous borders, the unchecked spread of narcotics, and the inability of gun control laws to impact criminals the United States finds itself increasingly vulnerable to the continued spread of cartel power. This power, underscored by violence and marked by a steady supply of illicit firearms, poses an existential threat to public safety, societal cohesion, and the very fabric of American communities.

Here, the free flow of drugs is contingent upon the ready supply of weapons, each fuelling the other in an endless cycle of death and profit.

European Cities: The Rise of Organised Gang Violence

The situation in Europe is alarmingly similar, with organised crime networks increasingly seizing control of urban areas, particularly in nations like Sweden, the Netherlands, and the UK. As stringent gun laws aim to curtail violence, these regulations have instead created a black-market catering exclusively to criminals who now control the underground trade. In recent years, Sweden has found itself engulfed in an extraordinary surge of gang-related violence, a phenomenon that has surprised many both within and outside its borders. Once considered a bastion of social stability and progressive policies, Sweden now faces the unsettling reality of rising crime rates and increasing brutality within its cities. This violence is not an isolated trend but rather a symptom of deeper issues specifically, the confluence of drug trafficking and illegal firearms smuggling that has allowed gang culture to take root and flourish in a society previously unaccustomed to such levels of unrest.

The Swedish government has responded by tightening legal access to firearms and enforcing more stringent restrictions for civilians to curtail violence. However, this approach has largely proven ineffective in addressing the root of the problem. The gangs responsible for this surge in violence are not bound by these legal restrictions; instead, they sidestep them entirely, obtaining their weapons through black-market channels. Despite the government's efforts to clamp down on lawful gun ownership, the availability of illicit firearms remains high, with firearms smuggled in from conflict zones and other high-risk regions across Europe and beyond. As a result, the gangs continue to access weaponry as readily as before, and the violence persists, a stark reminder that regulatory restrictions on law-abiding citizens do little to disarm those with criminal intent.

The situation in Sweden exemplifies the critical flaw in a gun control approach that fails to account for the realities of organised crime and smuggling networks. Swedish officials initially pursued a path of strict firearm regulation, assuming that reducing the number of legally owned guns would lessen opportunities for violence. Yet this approach overlooked a crucial detail: the gangs' firearms do not come from legal sources. These weapons flow into the country through an underground economy, facilitated by sophisticated smuggling networks that operate with virtual impunity across European borders. This is not a simple issue of domestic crime but rather an international problem, with guns sourced from regions with ongoing conflicts and trafficked through porous European borders a stark illustration of how global instability fuels local violence.

Compounding this issue is the role of drug trafficking, which acts as both the financial lifeline and primary motivator for gang activity. These gangs are not simply groups of disenfranchised youth; they are highly organised entities driven by profit and power, and the narcotics trade provides both in ample supply. With drug markets expanding and the demand for illicit substances ever-growing, gang networks have seized upon this opportunity, using violence and intimidation to establish control over their territories and assert dominance over rival groups. Firearms, in this context, are essential. They are the instruments through which these organisations enforce their will, secure their assets, and maintain their share of the lucrative drug market. Without guns, these gangs would struggle to uphold the power dynamics that underpin their existence; with them, they can enforce a form of brutal order within the communities they dominate.

For the average Swede, this wave of violence is a bitter shock, a sudden rupture in the social fabric that once defined the nation. Sweden has long prided itself on a low crime rate and a high standard of public safety. However, the presence of armed gangs has altered this landscape drastically. Cities like Stockholm, Gothenburg, and Malmö have seen spikes in shootings, grenade attacks, and other violent confrontations, a phenomenon alien to Sweden's recent history. The nation's gun laws, aimed at preventing precisely this kind of violence, have had little impact on the gangs' firepower, illustrating a painful paradox: while law-abiding citizens find themselves increasingly restricted in their ability to own and use firearms, criminal organisations operate seemingly without constraint, exploiting a thriving black market that disregards national borders and legal regulations entirely.

This situation raises an essential question about the efficacy of Sweden's gun control policies. It demonstrates, as seen in other contexts, that restricting legal access to firearms does not necessarily translate to a reduction in armed violence, especially when the primary perpetrators are not sourcing their weapons legally. Instead, it often results in a disparity in firepower between citizens and criminals, leaving communities vulnerable and policing forces stretched. Swedish law enforcement now faces an uphill battle, confronting not only the criminals themselves but also the extensive smuggling networks that bring illegal firearms into the country, networks that often prove too vast and elusive to dismantle with existing resources.

Indeed, Sweden's predicament highlights a larger European challenge. Borderless travel and trade, pillars of the European Union, have also inadvertently facilitated the movement of illicit goods, including firearms. As gun-smuggling routes crisscross the continent, linking conflict zones in Eastern Europe to the streets of Western cities, the challenge of controlling illegal firearms becomes increasingly complex. For nations like Sweden, whose own culture and policies have been shaped by ideals of peace and stability, grappling with this level of violence poses a significant social and political dilemma. The government's attempts to address it through restrictive gun policies have thus far shown limited results, leaving open questions about alternative approaches that might prove more effective.

Sweden's experience serves as a cautionary tale for other Western nations grappling with similar issues. As I've discussed in previous chapters, restrictive gun laws, while well-intentioned, often fail to address the true sources of criminal power, leaving citizens exposed to dangers that these laws were designed to prevent. The intertwining of drug trafficking and gun smuggling in Sweden highlights the need for policies that target the root causes of organised crime rather than focusing exclusively on restricting lawful firearm ownership. Without a coordinated effort to dismantle the networks that facilitate the flow of both drugs and illegal guns, Sweden and indeed, much of Europe may find itself facing a wave of criminality that its traditional policies are ill-equipped to handle.

Many European cities have transformed into contested zones, arenas where organised crime syndicates engage in an unrelenting struggle for dominance over highly profitable criminal enterprises. From the bustling ports of Rotterdam, one of the largest gateways for goods into Europe, to the streets of Malmö, where once-safe neighbourhoods now grapple with gang activity, the continent is seeing the direct effects of an underworld fuelled by the globalisation of crime. This battle for control over the lucrative drug market, human trafficking networks, and even arms smuggling has rendered European cities both staging grounds and battlegrounds for these criminal factions.

Rotterdam, as a major port city, is especially vulnerable to illicit trade. While it plays a crucial role in legal commerce, its vast infrastructure and heavy volume of goods make it an ideal target for those seeking to move contraband. Cartels and crime networks exploit these logistical complexities to smuggle in everything from narcotics to firearms, concealing illegal goods within otherwise legitimate shipments. The scale of trafficking operations here is staggering, with authorities often outpaced by the sheer ingenuity and resources of these syndicates. Drug seizures, while frequent, represent only a fraction of the actual volume flowing through the city's docks. Cocaine, for example, has become so prevalent that the port has earned a reputation as one of the key points of entry for the European cocaine trade. However, as quickly as enforcement agencies attempt to stem the tide, these organisations find new methods of import and distribution, continually evolving to evade capture.

In Malmö, the situation is emblematic of a growing crisis that affects smaller, less fortified cities as well. The city, like others in Sweden, has seen a stark rise in violent confrontations between gangs vying for dominance in drug trafficking and territorial control. Here, the same groups that profit from drug sales also exploit human trafficking, using vulnerable migrant populations as both victims and foot soldiers in their operations. The porous nature of Sweden's borders has allowed organised crime networks to gain a foothold, leading to a breakdown in public safety. Explosions, drive-by shootings, and gang-related murders have become grimly familiar in a country where such events were once unthinkable.

These syndicates do not operate in isolation but are instead part of larger, well-established networks that extend across multiple borders. Albanian, Moroccan, and Serbian groups, among others, have carved out territories within major cities across Europe, forming alliances and rivalries as they seek to control the supply chains of narcotics and other illegal commodities. This trend has turned neighbourhoods in cities like Brussels, Marseille, and Berlin into flashpoints of criminal violence, impacting residents and stretching the resources of law enforcement agencies. Each faction not only pursues its interests but also adapts its strategies in response to both local and international pressures, creating a constantly shifting landscape of crime.

The human trafficking component of these operations represents one of the darkest and most sinister aspects of this ongoing conflict. As outlined in my previous work, human trafficking has evolved into a highly lucrative industry, one that criminal organisations have perfected with ruthless efficiency. Many of the migrants smuggled into Europe under the promise of asylum or employment become trapped in a cycle of exploitation, forced into labour or prostitution to repay the "debts" they incurred during their journey. The ports and border towns serve as critical junctures in this process, where traffickers process and transfer their human cargo with chilling regularity. For every migrant who arrives seeking a better life, there are those whose futures are stolen by these networks, underscoring the human cost of unchecked organised crime.

Ironically, in many of these cities, restrictive firearm policies aimed at curbing violence among civilians have done little to reduce the arsenal available to criminal syndicates. Despite stringent laws, criminals continue to procure military-grade weaponry, exploiting smuggling channels that bypass regulatory checks. These weapons, often trafficked from conflict zones in Eastern Europe, end up in the hands of street-level enforcers and higher-ranking operatives alike. For example, in Brussels, French-manufactured assault rifles and Serbian handguns are common finds during police raids, underscoring the scale and sophistication of smuggling networks that stretch across the continent. In effect, the illegal firearms market complements the narcotics trade, as guns are not only tools of intimidation and enforcement but also a currency of exchange in the underworld economy.

For residents of these cities, the effects are both tangible and terrifying. In neighbourhoods where gang violence has become part of daily life, parents fear for their children, and businesses suffer under the shadow of extortion and vandalism. Even more insidious is the gradual erosion of trust in law enforcement and public institutions. Citizens, disillusioned by the seemingly endless cycle of crime and violence, begin to question the ability of their governments to protect them. This crisis of confidence is compounded when the authorities impose firearm restrictions on civilians without adequately addressing the weapons in the hands of criminals. Consequently, communities feel disempowered and abandoned, left to navigate the complexities of crime and insecurity with limited means of self-defence or recourse.

The organised crime syndicates responsible for this violence are also remarkably resilient, leveraging modern technology, corruption, and international alliances to sustain and expand their operations. Their sophisticated use of encrypted communications, coupled with their ability to bribe or intimidate officials, allows them to evade detection and enforcement with alarming success. In some cases, these networks have established connections with corrupt elements within law enforcement or border control, further complicating efforts to dismantle their operations. It is a brutal irony that the very systems meant to uphold the rule of law are occasionally compromised by the very criminals they seek to apprehend.

The European response to this crisis has been piecemeal at best. While there are instances of collaboration between nations, such as joint operations targeting major smuggling routes, these efforts often lack the consistency and cohesion needed to make a lasting impact. Criminal organisations exploit these gaps in coordination, moving from one jurisdiction to another with relative ease. The criminal networks operate on a global scale, yet much of the law enforcement response remains hampered by national limitations, fragmented approaches, and bureaucracy. Thus, as criminal enterprises continue to evolve and expand, European nations find themselves increasingly outpaced, unable to mount a unified and effective countermeasure.

Ultimately, the battle waged in Europe's cities between criminal syndicates is a symptom of deeper issues, including lax border controls, fragmented law enforcement, and, crucially, a failure to address the economic and social conditions that allow organised crime to thrive. Unless these underlying factors are confronted, we risk witnessing an ever-worsening cycle of violence and instability, with the boundaries between legal and illegal markets, and between public and private security, becoming dangerously blurred. In these battleground cities, the ordinary citizen pays the heaviest price, caught in a struggle, not of their making but one from which they have little escape.

The violence is no longer confined to the underworld but increasingly spills into residential neighbourhoods, impacting civilians who often feel trapped between inadequate law enforcement and ruthless criminal networks. The availability of illegal firearms, often trafficked from Eastern Europe or repurposed military weapons from conflict zones, is a primary driver of this violence. Gangs and crime syndicates within Europe are now arming themselves with sophistication and firepower previously unseen, their operations effectively shielded by restrictive gun laws that disarm citizens and thereby enhance criminal control over entire districts.

The Failures of Gun Control Policies in a Changing Criminal Landscape

In examining the modern landscape of gun control, a troubling realisation emerges: current policies are rooted primarily in ideology, imposing increasingly onerous conditions on law-abiding citizens while neglecting to effectively penalise the criminal use of firearms. Governments in both the USA and Europe have approached gun control with a focus on restricting civilian ownership, under the assumption that limiting access to firearms will naturally reduce violence. Yet, these laws fail to account for a critical and inconvenient truth: criminal organisations whether they be local gangs or vast transnational cartels are not bound by such regulations. Instead, these policies unintentionally disarm the very people they purport to protect while leaving criminals and their enterprises remarkably well-equipped.

This ideological approach to gun control reveals a fundamental disconnect between policy intentions and on-the-ground realities. While restrictive laws are enacted in the name of public safety, they are, in effect, creating environments where law-abiding citizens are less able to defend themselves against the increasingly armed criminal elements that permeate our societies. In cities with strict gun regulations places like Chicago in the USA or London in the UK violent crime has surged, with offenders obtaining firearms through illegal channels that gun control laws do little to obstruct. As I have explored in prior chapters, we see this same pattern in European cities like Malmö, Rotterdam, and Brussels, where gangs and organised crime syndicates have no difficulty accessing weapons, even as civilians face ever-stricter limits on their rights to self-defence.

This disconnect stems, in part, from a simplistic belief that controlling legal gun ownership will somehow deter illegal acquisition and usage. However, criminals do not acquire firearms through registered dealers or legal channels; they obtain them through underground markets that operate irrespective of regulatory frameworks. As gun control policies become stricter, these underground markets only grow in sophistication, adapting to meet the increased demand from those who operate outside the law. The tightening of legal gun ownership can inadvertently strengthen these black markets, as criminals exploit the demand gap created by restrictive policies. The result is an imbalance where those willing to break the law enjoy unfettered access to weapons, while ordinary citizens face increasingly limited options for protecting themselves.

The USA provides a compelling case study of this phenomenon. Alongside the country's efforts to impose gun control laws in cities like Chicago, we see staggering levels of gun crime, not by law-abiding owners but by criminals who remain entirely unaffected by regulatory measures. Many of these weapons are trafficked into urban areas from other regions with fewer restrictions, illustrating that localised gun control is a weak deterrent to organised crime. Cartels, with their deeply entrenched networks across North and Central America, have transformed smuggling into a fine-tuned industry, bringing firearms across borders as readily as they transport drugs. Yet, instead of addressing this international pipeline, policymakers continue to focus on civilian restrictions within their borders, a strategy that largely misses the mark.

Europe's approach similarly illustrates the limitations of ideology-driven policy. The UK, for example, has one of the strictest gun control frameworks in the world, implemented with the intention to reduce firearm-related violence. Yet, violent crime, especially knife and gun crime, has risen significantly in recent years, suggesting that the core problem lies elsewhere. Criminal organisations in the UK have ready access to firearms, smuggled in from countries with more relaxed regulations or trafficked from conflict zones in Eastern Europe. These weapons enter the UK through the same clandestine routes that serve the drug trade, fuelling a cycle of violence that gun control policies fail to disrupt. The irony is stark: ordinary citizens are restricted from owning firearms even for self-defence, while criminal networks face few such impediments.

As I have discussed previously, this asymmetry places citizens at a distinct disadvantage. By imposing increasingly strict regulations on firearm ownership, governments are not only limiting personal freedom but also diminishing the public's ability to safeguard themselves in a climate of rising criminality. In essence, citizens are made more vulnerable, while those who operate outside the law capitalise on this vulnerability. Many policymakers seem unwilling to confront this uncomfortable reality, choosing instead to perpetuate the belief that disarming civilians equates to safer societies. Yet, as the evidence from both the USA and Europe reveals, this approach leaves communities exposed, with fewer practical means of protection.

Moreover, the failure to severely penalise the criminal use of firearms further compounds this issue. Current policies often focus on preventing civilian ownership rather than aggressively pursuing criminal misuse. In many cases, those who use firearms in violent crimes face penalties that fail to serve as an effective deterrent. This soft-handed approach to punishment sends a problematic message: that society is more concerned with regulating the law-abiding than with punishing the law-breakers. The inconsistency is apparent, as violent offenders are repeatedly released back into communities after serving minimal sentences, often to re-offend with relative impunity. This leniency stands in stark contrast to the rigidity applied to lawful gun owners, many of whom face arduous requirements just to maintain their right to self-defence.

This dynamic also erodes trust between citizens and their governments. When ordinary people see policies that appear more focused on regulating their freedoms than on curbing criminal violence, faith in public institutions wanes. Communities become sceptical of policies that seem divorced from their lived experiences and disconnected from the realities of modern criminality. People begin to question whether their safety is truly the priority, or if policymakers are more interested in appearing ideologically consistent than in making genuine strides towards public security. As long as governments continue to equate stringent gun control with crime prevention, without addressing the real factors behind organised crime and illegal firearm circulation, the policy framework remains fundamentally flawed.

In light of this, we must consider an approach that goes beyond ideology and addresses the hard truths of today's criminal landscape. Effective gun control, if it is to exist, should include measures that specifically target the black markets that supply weapons to organised crime. This approach would involve stricter penalties for firearm smuggling, enhanced cross-border cooperation to dismantle trafficking networks, and a concerted effort to enforce laws against violent offenders. Rather than disarming law-abiding citizens, a more balanced approach would empower them to protect themselves while focusing enforcement where it truly matters: on those who would use firearms to terrorise and exploit communities.

Ultimately, the aim should be to create a society where citizens feel both protected and empowered, free from the threat of violence without sacrificing their right to self-defence. As long as governments cling to ideologically driven gun control policies, they risk exacerbating the very issues they claim to address, leaving organised criminals well-armed and ordinary citizens defenceless. It is a balance that policymakers must strive to achieve, for without it, the cycle of violence will continue, and the burden of crime will fall disproportionately on those least equipped to bear it.

The failure of these policies lies in their inability to address the supply chains that make firearms accessible to criminals. While gun control advocates argue that restrictions on firearms will curb violence, the evidence suggests that such measures merely create a disparity, where the balance of power is tipped decidedly in favour of those willing to operate outside the law.

Community Impact: Lives Lived in Fear

As I delve into the intricate nexus between criminality and gun control, a troubling realisation takes shape: modern gun control policies, rooted largely in ideological premises, have been crafted with the notion that reducing civilian firearm access will somehow stymie violence. These policies, however, tend to focus overwhelmingly on placing stringent conditions on lawful ownership onerous and exacting requirements for ordinary citizens. Meanwhile, these very laws appear blind to a critical truth: criminal enterprises, from local street gangs to sprawling transnational cartels, remain unshackled by these regulations. The legislation, in effect, is primarily felt by those who seek to abide by it, creating a paradox where the law-abiding are disarmed and increasingly vulnerable, while criminal entities continue to thrive, well-armed and emboldened.

What stands out is the ideological underpinning of these gun control policies. They are often championed as measures to ensure public safety, but they are largely directed at reducing legal firearm ownership. From my research and exploration across previous chapters, particularly in dissecting the ramifications of mass migration and open borders on arms trafficking, it becomes clear that the current framework has little impact on the very segments it seeks to curb. Instead of tackling the sources of illegal firearms be they smuggling rings, black markets, or clandestine manufacturing operations the focus remains squarely on legal avenues. The result is that these policies inadvertently restrict only those citizens who seek to follow the law, leaving criminal organisations whether organised crime syndicates in Europe or drug cartels in the USA free to procure and wield weapons with alarming ease.

In Europe, the disconnect between restrictive gun laws and the reality of criminal access to firearms is particularly stark. The UK serves as a prime example, with some of the strictest gun control measures in the world. Despite this, violent crime persists unabated, with firearms and knives flooding into the hands of criminals through underground networks that circumvent domestic laws altogether. These weapons often originate from Eastern European countries or conflict zones where gun control is lax, making them readily available to those willing to exploit these channels. As I noted in my previous analysis, the ports of Rotterdam and Antwerp are key conduits in this underground arms trade, allowing gangs and traffickers to obtain firearms that would otherwise be inaccessible through legal means. In focusing on restricting legal ownership, policymakers have largely ignored these routes, inadvertently fostering a climate where criminals are better armed than the citizens they prey upon.

In the USA, too, this ideological approach has seen cities with strict gun control laws, such as Chicago, consistently report some of the highest rates of gun violence. Here again, we witness the same failure to adapt policy to the shifting dynamics of criminal enterprises. Gun control advocates in these cities argue that tighter restrictions will reduce violence, yet the statistics tell a different story. Illegal firearms continue to pour in, often trafficked from states with more lenient gun laws or brought over the US-Mexico border, where cartels have honed smuggling into a sophisticated, industrial-scale operation. Rather than addressing the pipeline of illicit firearms into cities, the laws instead focus on making legal ownership increasingly difficult, leaving law-abiding citizens with limited options for self-defence. Meanwhile, cartels and local gangs acquire weapons that allow them to consolidate power, intimidate communities, and ensure control over lucrative drug territories, all without facing the same constraints that govern the average citizen.

This situation reflects a fundamental miscalculation by policymakers: that restricting civilian access to firearms will make society safer. But as we see time and time again, criminal organisations are not constrained by legalities. They operate within parallel economies, outside the reach of conventional regulation, where the availability of firearms is dictated not by laws but by supply, demand, and profitability. For these groups, firearms are essential tools not just for personal protection, but as instruments of business enforcement and territorial control. In both the USA and Europe, gangs and cartels rely on their arsenals to protect assets, deter rivals, and command loyalty. By restricting firearms for civilians while failing to inhibit access for criminals, governments have created an environment in which those willing to break the law hold a distinct advantage over those who seek to uphold it.

The ideological roots of modern gun control policies also bring about a severe imbalance in enforcement. While the law's weight bears down on lawful gun owners through exhaustive checks, fees, and ownership limitations, it often fails to adequately penalise the criminal misuse of firearms. For instance, sentencing for firearm-related crimes can vary widely, with repeat offenders frequently receiving lenient penalties or parole, allowing them to return to communities with minimal repercussions. This sends a message that society is more focused on curbing the rights of responsible citizens than it is on addressing the actions of those who misuse weapons to perpetrate violence.

This incongruity between law-abiding citizens facing strict ownership conditions and criminals operating with impunity ultimately fosters a deep-seated sense of insecurity among the public. People in both the USA and Europe are left questioning the effectiveness of policies that seem more intent on constraining them than on holding violent offenders accountable. This has led, in part, to growing disillusionment with governments' ability to safeguard their communities, with citizens increasingly sceptical of laws that do little to address the root of violence while making self-defence a bureaucratic hurdle. It is difficult for citizens to trust that they are truly protected when the law effectively removes their means of defence while appearing to tolerate, even indirectly enabling, the empowerment of criminals.

In my book, *"The Empire's Warning: What Rome's Fall Tells Us About the West Today"*, I discussed the parallel with Roman governance, where a failure to address the root causes of societal ills eventually weakened the state's relationship with its people. Much like Rome's increasingly ineffective legislation, modern gun control measures often serve as symbolic gestures, offering the semblance of action without tackling the underlying issues. Just as the Roman Empire found itself unable to defend its borders or its citizens in the face of growing external and internal threats, today's policies risk leaving Western societies exposed. Unless the focus shifts from symbolic regulation to practical, enforceable actions that target criminal enterprises directly, we risk perpetuating a status quo that benefits no one except, of course, the very criminal elements these policies are ostensibly meant to combat.

What is required, then, is a pragmatic approach that prioritises effectiveness over ideology, one that recognises that disarming law-abiding citizens while leaving criminals armed is a flawed strategy. Rather than rigidly restricting civilian ownership, governments must shift focus to dismantling the underground markets that feed firearms to criminals, enhance penalties for gun-related crimes, and build cross-border coalitions to intercept weapons before they reach criminal networks. Only by addressing these systemic issues can we hope to craft policies that protect citizens without sacrificing their rights a balance that, if achieved, could reverse the troubling trend of communities left defenceless while criminals flourish.

This evolution in policy would reflect an acknowledgement that a one-size-fits-all approach to gun control, one that punishes the law-abiding without deterring the lawless, has outlived its relevance in today's complex, interconnected criminal landscape. The path forward demands that we approach gun control not as an ideological battleground but as a practical matter of public safety, one that serves to restore the balance of power to those it was always meant to protect: the people.

Consequently, law-abiding citizens find themselves effectively disarmed and vulnerable, while criminal organisations operate with ever-increasing boldness.

A Triad Too Deeply Rooted?

The triad of guns, drugs, and organised crime has established itself as a fixture within the fabric of modern society, creating a cycle of violence and fear that seems impervious to traditional regulatory measures. As governments focus on disarming citizens in the hope of reducing crime, they overlook the broader structural and economic factors that enable organised crime to flourish. Gun control policies, while ostensibly aimed at reducing violence, have inadvertently made communities less secure by disempowering citizens and emboldening criminals. Without addressing the interconnected nature of these criminal enterprises, any attempt to curb violence and protect communities will ultimately prove inadequate.

In the final analysis, breaking this triad demands not only stricter regulation but a comprehensive strategy that tackles the root causes of organised crime. Targeting the flow of firearms alone will achieve little without addressing the demand for narcotics, the structures that sustain organised crime, and the economic conditions that drive individuals into these enterprises. We face a critical juncture where we must reassess not only our policies on gun control but also our broader approach to law enforcement and community protection. Only by understanding the complex interplay of guns, drugs, and organised crime can we begin to unravel this web and restore a sense of security and agency to the very communities that have suffered the most.

Chapter 5: Undermining Law Enforcement: The Impact of Defunding and Policy Shifts

In recent years, the concept of "defunding the police" has evolved from a rallying cry into a concrete policy decision across several Western cities, most notably in the United States, but also, increasingly, in parts of Europe. What began as a push for accountability has, in practice, led to a reallocation of funds away from law enforcement, often to social programmes or community-based initiatives intended to address the root causes of crime. The idea, at least in its idealistic form, was to reimagine public safety in a way that emphasised social support over traditional policing, addressing what proponents see as systemic inequalities within the criminal justice system.

Yet, as I have found through researching recent trends and considering their historical context, the consequences have often proved far more complex and far-reaching than anticipated. Like many policies rooted in a mixture of well-intentioned and ideological desires, the concept of police defunding touches upon fundamental issues of security, governance, and social cohesion concerns that resonate through the foundations of Western societies and raise profound questions about the role of the state in protecting its citizens.

In this chapter, I will explore how police defunding, combined with shifts in law enforcement policy, has impacted both the enforcement of gun laws and the broader safety of citizens. Drawing upon case studies, insights from criminologists, perspectives from police unions, and data from cities that have adopted significant budget cuts, I will attempt to shed light on the ripple effects of these changes. The aim is not simply to catalogue the consequences but to examine the broader societal and criminal justice implications, where we increasingly see public safety caught in the crossfire of ideological movements and political shifts. In previous works, I examined the lessons drawn from the past, and here I will continue to explore these parallels, particularly looking at the potential degradation of civic institutions when weakened by reactionary reforms rather than balanced, measured evolution.

Defunding: Ideals Versus Realities

The modern defunding movement has its origins in a range of grievances, including perceptions of systemic injustice and historical inequalities within the policing system. What makes this movement so significant, however, is its rapid transformation from protest slogans to actual policy changes, particularly in American cities like Minneapolis, Portland, and New York. Here, we see budgets reduced by millions of dollars, often reallocated to social services intending to address what some refer to as the "root causes" of crime. This shift, however, comes at the expense of core law enforcement functions, leading to notable and troubling consequences.

In past research, notably while writing on the decline of Rome in *The Empire's Warning: What Rome's Fall Tells Us About the West Today*, I explored how weakened state institutions paved the way for societal disorder and vulnerability to external threats. Rome's diminished capacity to maintain law and order within its borders left it increasingly exposed to incursions, internal conflicts, and eventual fragmentation. In a comparable vein, the reduction in policing resources today seems to have similarly emboldened criminal networks, especially in regions where gang and cartel activities have capitalised on the absence of a strong law enforcement presence. For example, recent crime data from American cities with substantial budget cuts reveal sharp rises in violent crime suggesting that when law enforcement weakens, those who thrive in lawlessness seize the opportunity.

The Rise of Defunding: Context and Catalysts

The call to "defund the police" is not simply a slogan; it has come to symbolise a profound and escalating distrust towards law enforcement institutions in certain urban areas. In the United States, this movement gained traction in the wake of several high-profile incidents involving police violence, which were fomented by a left-leaning press and government and sparked national outrage and a wave of protests. These events fuelled demands for substantial reforms, underscoring a widespread perception of systemic issues within the policing system. There is little question that some reform is indeed necessary, particularly in areas where transparency, accountability, and community relations have suffered. However, the sweeping budget cuts implemented in response have, in many cases, extended beyond reallocating resources to community programmes and mental health initiatives, leading instead to a profound weakening of police capabilities.

Reflecting upon the historical precedents discussed in *The Empire's Warning: What Rome's Fall Tells Us About the West Today*, I see troubling parallels between the current wave of defunding and Rome's struggles with resource allocation in its later years. Rome, faced with social unrest and political pressures, began diverting resources away from its core defence and public order institutions. Over time, this contributed to its inability to manage internal disorder, exposing its citizens to lawlessness and leaving its borders vulnerable to external threats. The budget cuts in American cities like Minneapolis, Portland, and New York bear some resemblance to this phenomenon, as millions of dollars have been reallocated away from police departments under the banner of reform. While the motivations behind these actions may differ, the outcomes of strained resources, limited personnel, and a subsequent rise in criminal activity echo the missteps of Rome's leadership during its decline.

The impact of these reductions on law enforcement agencies has been profound. Police departments, already struggling to balance the demands of a complex and often hostile public environment, now face a diminished capacity to respond effectively to crime. In Minneapolis, where cuts were particularly severe, the department was left with fewer officers on the streets, reducing their presence in vulnerable neighbourhoods. Portland and New York have also seen similar reductions, resulting in limitations on officer availability and a concerning decline in training resources, essential for maintaining professionalism and accountability within the ranks. The scarcity of vital equipment and advanced technologies further compounds these issues, leaving officers ill-equipped to handle increasingly sophisticated criminal networks.

In previous chapters, I argued that policing and public safety rely on a balance between resource adequacy and accountability. To ensure both, law enforcement must be supported not undermined if they are to effectively uphold the law and protect citizens. With fewer resources, the ability of these cities to address rising violent crime has been notably compromised. For instance, reports from Minneapolis and Portland indicate a measurable increase in homicides and assaults, reflecting the unintended consequences of resource depletion. The disconnect between idealistic aspirations for community-based safety and the practical requirements of law enforcement becomes starkly evident here. Community programmes alone, while valuable, cannot replace the deterrent and protective presence that police departments provide, nor can they address the immediate need to respond to violent crime effectively.

The experience of these cities underscores critical questions about the efficacy and long-term impact of defunding. Can a society realistically expect a well-functioning public safety system if it continually depletes the resources that enable its effectiveness? I would argue that the answer, as history has shown us, is no. The erosion of law enforcement capabilities may offer short-term political appeasement, but it ultimately jeopardises the safety and security of the very communities it purports to protect. In "*The Empire's Warning*," I emphasised that a functional society depends upon stable, well-resourced institutions; without these, the foundations of order, trust, and security begin to crumble.

In Europe, while the concept of "defunding the police" has not swept across the continent as it has in the United States, there has been a discernible shift towards what some have termed "policing with restraint." This approach, often guided by political pressures and public opinion, prioritises reducing confrontational tactics and limiting certain enforcement practices deemed too invasive or authoritarian. The intent, largely well-meaning, is to avoid inflaming tensions with communities already distrustful of police presence. Yet, in practice, this trend has frequently led to a policing style that emphasises optics over effective crime deterrence. In parts of the UK and France, for example, this strategy has resulted in a visible stretching of resources, as limited personnel and budgets are directed towards containing the visible symptoms of social issues rather than tackling the deep-rooted causes of unrest and criminality.

Reflecting on historical parallels, I am reminded of how Rome's later rulers, in a bid to placate the populace and avoid inciting unrest, reduced their reliance on proactive enforcement and centralised security. This policy shift, intended to ease public discontent, ultimately weakened Rome's internal stability and exposed its citizens to greater risks. Today's European cities, notably London, Paris, and Marseille, may face a similar dilemma. Rather than empowering law enforcement to confront criminal elements head-on, they are adopting softer, less confrontational approaches that risk emboldening organised criminal elements and gang networks, particularly in urban areas already grappling with high levels of gang activity and illegal arms.

Take, for example, the changes to "stop and search" policies within the UK. In recent years, concerns over civil liberties and accusations of racial profiling have led to significant reductions in the use of this tactic. While these adjustments aim to protect individual rights, they have also had unintended consequences for public safety. As previously mentioned, tools like stop and search, though controversial, are often crucial for intercepting illegal firearms and other contraband. The evidence indicates a correlation between the reduction in these interventions and a rise in gun violence, particularly in areas where gang activity is prevalent. London, where stop and search has been severely curtailed, has witnessed increasing difficulties in tracking illegal arms, a concerning trend that mirrors the challenges American cities face when police presence is reduced.

France, too, faces its version of this problem. With an increasingly diverse and urbanised population, the country has been cautious about deploying aggressive policing tactics in volatile suburban areas, particularly where there are long-standing social tensions. In recent years, French authorities have been urged to adopt a less confrontational approach, focusing on de-escalation rather than assertive intervention. However, in cities like Marseille, where gang violence and organised crime flourish, this policy shift has often left law enforcement scrambling to contain violence without the necessary tools and political backing. The reluctance to engage forcefully with organised criminal groups has not only allowed these networks to thrive but has also contributed to a climate of impunity that jeopardises public security.

This balance between upholding civil rights and ensuring public safety remains a particularly delicate and contentious issue. While the goals of civil rights and fair treatment in policing are undoubtedly essential, the challenge lies in preserving these values without compromising the ability of law enforcement to safeguard communities. The dilemma of prioritising placation over enforcement was a choice that ultimately weakened Rome's resilience against both internal and external threats. Europe, with its focus on restraint in law enforcement, risks a similar fate if it continues to prioritise avoiding public backlash over addressing the growing threats within its borders.

The result is a police force that is increasingly under-resourced and often demoralised, as the demands on officers outstrip the means provided to meet them. The difficulties in achieving this delicate balance have broader implications, not only for immediate security but also for the social contract that underpins public trust in institutions. As European societies grapple with evolving urban and social landscapes, they must recognise the potential long-term risks of undercutting the tools and authority that law enforcement needs to address rising criminality.

Strain on Law Enforcement: Consequences of Reduced Funding and Restrictive Policies

The direct consequences of reduced police budgets are indeed multifaceted, yet one of the most immediate and troubling impacts is on the enforcement of gun laws. To uphold and apply existing firearms legislation effectively, police departments require a robust infrastructure of manpower, resources, and strategic planning. In the absence of adequate funding, the capacity to enforce these laws is severely compromised, leaving communities more vulnerable to the very violence that these laws aim to curb. In previous chapters, I explored this paradox: cities with the strictest gun laws, such as Chicago, are simultaneously besieged by some of the highest rates of gun violence. This irony serves as a stark reminder of the limitations that law enforcement faces under the constraints of defunded models.

Chicago, where gun violence has plagued neighbourhoods for years, offers a striking illustration of the dangers posed by slashing police budgets. Police departments here have been forced to cut back on officers in high-crime areas, resulting in diminished patrols in precisely the places that need them most. The presence of an officer can act as a deterrent, both to petty crimes and to more serious offences involving firearms. Without a visible and active police presence, however, the deterrent effect dissipates, emboldening those who might otherwise be more cautious. Criminals are quick to capitalise on this void, aware that the probability of apprehension has diminished alongside the reduction in police coverage.

Furthermore, reduced budgets impact not only the number of officers on the street but also the quality of the investigative processes within police departments. Proactively addressing illegal gun trafficking, identifying networks, and pursuing those responsible for supplying weapons to gangs and other criminal entities require specialised units, ongoing surveillance, and technological resources all of which demand funding. With budget cuts, departments must often divert resources from specialised units to general patrols or other critical needs, diluting their ability to tackle complex issues like gun trafficking. Consequently, these budgetary constraints create an environment in which illegal firearms flow unchecked into high-crime communities, with little capacity to track, seize, or trace the weapons back to their sources.

In *The Empire's Warning: What Rome's Fall Tells Us About the West Today*, I explored a similar theme, examining how Rome, in its later years, reduced its patrols and military oversight in certain border territories, unintentionally creating a power vacuum. Just as frontier settlements were left exposed to threats without adequate military support, today's cities are left vulnerable to an influx of illegal firearms when police departments cannot control and interdict these flows. The unsettling parallel highlights that underfunded enforcement mechanisms serve as open invitations for criminal networks to thrive, leaving ordinary citizens at the mercy of unchecked violence.

Moreover, gun law enforcement under a defunded model faces another critical obstacle: reduced funding for preventative community-based initiatives that work in conjunction with law enforcement. Policing is not a purely reactive enterprise; many departments have worked in recent years to develop partnerships with communities to prevent violence, intervene early, and engage at-risk individuals before they turn to gun crime. However, budget cuts often mean that community outreach programmes, public safety workshops, and preventive policing initiatives are among the first to be curtailed. This narrowing of focus leaves law enforcement with fewer avenues for reducing crime through non-confrontational means, forcing them into a reactive role that is less effective and, ultimately, more costly in both resources and human lives.

Chicago's struggles are mirrored in other American cities facing similar cuts, where the idealistic vision of reallocating police budgets to other community resources often lacks the practical infrastructure to address violent crime. Despite having some of the most stringent gun laws in the United States, cities like Los Angeles, Baltimore, and New York are also witnessing alarming increases in gun violence. While these laws are intended to prevent firearms from falling into the wrong hands, laws alone are meaningless without the enforcement capacity to uphold them. As police budgets are slashed, the implementation of these laws is inevitably compromised. Fewer arrests are made, fewer firearms are seized, and fewer trafficking networks are dismantled, creating a dangerous feedback loop where weak enforcement fuels more crime, which in turn erodes public trust and places additional strain on an already overstretched system.

Thus, the situation reveals a harsh reality: stringent gun laws without robust enforcement capabilities only serve to underline the impotence of those laws. Stripping police departments of the resources they need to tackle gun violence directly undermines public safety and the ability of law enforcement to serve and protect. The result, as evidenced in these cities, is an erosion of public trust, a sense of insecurity among residents, and a steadily worsening spiral of crime that underfunded police forces are increasingly powerless to control. The lessons here are clear and urgent: without adequate resources, even the best-intentioned legislation becomes nothing more than an empty promise.

The Role of Police Unions and Public Safety Experts

Police unions have emerged as some of the most vocal and steadfast opponents of the defunding movement and the restrictive policies that have followed in its wake, insisting that effective policing cannot be achieved without the necessary resources, training, and support. To their point, policing is not a job that merely relies on the goodwill or resilience of its officers; it is a structured institution that demands continuous investment in equipment, personnel, and infrastructure. Representatives from unions in cities that have suffered defunding argue that the lack of resources has placed officers in precarious situations. They are expected to respond to violent and unpredictable crimes while lacking the manpower, equipment, or even the critical intelligence to do so safely or effectively.

In the United States, the National Fraternal Order of Police (NFOP), one of the largest police unions, has been particularly vocal in highlighting these issues. The union consistently points out that defunding has not just compromised the safety of officers, who are now working in increasingly dangerous conditions but has also exacerbated the risks faced by the general public. Officers are now frequently outnumbered and outgunned, expected to confront organised criminal elements without the tools that once empowered them to do so. As the NFOP has stressed, defunding is not merely an economic issue but a fundamental safety issue, and one that the public often underestimates until its effects are felt firsthand.

Public safety experts echo these concerns, noting that the effects of these policies extend far beyond police forces and reach into the very heart of communities, especially those already vulnerable to crime. In cities across the United States, high-crime neighbourhoods have been hit hardest by the decreased police presence resulting from budget cuts. Paradoxically, many of the loudest advocates for police defunding hail from low-crime or affluent areas where law enforcement is less visible in everyday life. These areas, often insulated from the consequences of such policies, have not felt the ripple effects of reduced policing with the same immediacy as communities in inner-city neighbourhoods, where crime rates are high and where police presence once played a crucial role in keeping violence at bay.

In these high-crime areas, the absence of proactive policing has led to a surge in gun-related incidents and other violent crimes. Local leaders and community representatives have spoken out, often with a sense of frustration, about the erosion of public security in their neighbourhoods. They report that their residents are now left feeling unprotected and increasingly wary of leaving their homes, especially at night. The irony is palpable: while budget cuts were intended to address grievances about police overreach, they have left some of the most crime-affected communities in a state of abandonment, caught between rising crime and reduced police intervention.

Defunding in a European Context: Political Pressures and Public Security

While defunding on the scale seen in the United States has not fully taken root in Europe, the political pressures leading to restrictive policing policies have nevertheless had a noticeable effect. The UK, for instance, has witnessed a series of cutbacks to police funding since the austerity measures following the 2008 financial crisis. Although these were not necessarily rooted in the same ideological grounds as the defunding movement in the United States, the result has been a similar erosion in police effectiveness. Police forces across the UK have been required to do more with less, managing rising crime rates with limited personnel and resources.

In addition, European countries face unique challenges associated with organised crime and terrorism, which often require specialised training, intelligence, and robust interagency cooperation. Yet, as resources are allocated towards visible public service priorities, there is less funding available for these vital, though less visible, areas of policing. In countries like France and Sweden, where gang violence and illegal firearm circulation have escalated in recent years, law enforcement agencies are increasingly stretched thin, struggling to respond to rising criminal activity with insufficient manpower.

The Unintended Impact on Gun Control

Perhaps one of the most paradoxical aspects of the defunding movement is its effect on gun control. In theory, stringent gun laws are designed to restrict the flow of firearms and reduce gun violence, but these laws rely on active enforcement to be effective. When law enforcement agencies are under-resourced and constrained by policy, enforcing gun regulations becomes an arduous, if not impossible, task. The illegal proliferation of firearms continues unchecked, driven by organised crime and international trafficking networks, while law-abiding citizens are left in a position of heightened vulnerability.

As we saw in earlier chapters, the intersection of open borders, mass migration, and illegal firearms trafficking has created a situation where guns are readily available to those who seek them on the black market. However, under a defunded law enforcement model, agencies tasked with controlling these illegal flows are simply outmatched. This leaves communities exposed to the repercussions of unchecked gun trafficking and organised criminal activity.

A Cautionary Tale

Ultimately, the trend of defunding the police represents a cautionary tale about the complexities of public safety policy. While there is no doubt that reform is necessary and that some policing practices are overdue for scrutiny, the wholesale reduction of law enforcement resources without a viable alternative has proven detrimental to the communities most in need of protection. In this era of rising crime, gang activity, and gun proliferation, defunding initiatives have, paradoxically, placed public safety in jeopardy, especially for those communities that cannot afford private security or other forms of protection.

This chapter underscores a crucial truth: public safety is, at its core, a shared responsibility that requires both resources and balance.

Policymakers must consider the long-term impact of defunding and restrictive policies, lest we find ourselves in a society where criminal elements operate unchecked, law-abiding citizens are left unprotected, and the very institutions tasked with upholding the law are left in a weakened state.

Chapter 6: Weapons of War: The Growth of Military-Grade Firearms in Criminal Hands

In recent years, we've witnessed a disquieting trend: the infiltration of military-grade firearms into the hands of criminal organisations. No longer content with simple handguns or shotguns, today's crime syndicates and street gangs are wielding weapons that one might expect to see in the hands of military personnel rather than local criminals. This chapter delves into how these high-powered firearms have reached criminal groups, the consequences for public safety and law enforcement, and the unintended outcomes of restrictive gun control laws that, while aiming to limit access for civilians, have left an opening for sophisticated weaponry in the hands of those who operate beyond the law.

The growth of this dangerous phenomenon is largely due to global black-market supply chains and porous borders. The unrestricted flow of arms through international black markets, coupled with weak border controls, has created a nearly seamless pipeline that delivers weapons into urban and rural areas alike. I'll explore the mechanics of these supply chains, the means through which these firearms are acquired, and the impact of these weapons on communities. In cases from both the United States and Europe, I'll highlight incidents where local police forces have encountered criminal elements equipped with far superior weaponry than they possess, underscoring the alarming reality that, in certain instances, law enforcement is outgunned.

The Rise of Military-Grade Weapons in Criminal Hands

The growth of military-grade firearms within criminal groups is not a trend confined to any single nation. Across borders, we're witnessing an alarming influx of weapons that were once the sole province of military forces, from assault rifles to explosives. In Mexico, for example, drug cartels have established a formidable arsenal that includes AR-15s, AK-47s, and even Barrett .50-calibre sniper rifles, capable of piercing armour and wreaking havoc on police vehicles. These firearms cross the US border with remarkable frequency, making their way into American cities and fuelling violence in areas already plagued by organised crime. Such high-powered rifles enable criminals to engage in violent confrontations with law enforcement, tipping the balance of power.

In Europe, the situation is no less dire, particularly with the influence of Eastern European black markets. Kalashnikov-style AK-47s, in both fully automatic and semi-automatic variants, are among the most trafficked weapons in Western Europe. These rifles, originally designed for war zones, are both durable and relatively easy to maintain, making them a prized asset for gangs. In France, for example, police have seized countless Kalashnikovs from urban gangs, particularly in cities like Marseille, where organised crime has wielded these weapons to enforce control over drug trafficking routes and territory. The AK-47, with its 7.62mm rounds, is devastating at short range, giving these groups a substantial tactical advantage over police who are limited to sidearms or, at most, standard-issue shotguns.

In the United Kingdom, firearms laws are notoriously strict, but this has not prevented military-grade weapons from slipping into criminal circles. London police have reported a steady rise in the appearance of semi-automatic rifles such as AR-15s and high-capacity 9mm pistols, such as Glock 17s, that can be modified to hold extended magazines. While full automatics are rare, they allow rapid firing of hundreds of rounds per minute, providing criminals with substantial firepower that can easily overwhelm the typical response from law enforcement. Just a decade ago, it would have been almost unthinkable for gangs to possess these sorts of weapons. However, with black-market channels expanding and criminal networks growing more resourceful, the arrival of high-capacity pistols, which can hold up to 33 rounds, and rapid-fire rifles have become disturbingly common.

Beyond rifles and pistols, European authorities are encountering more specialised weapons traditionally associated with military units, such as the M4 carbine, a standard-issue firearm for American forces that has now become a fixture in certain criminal arsenals. The M4, with its compact frame and ability to switch between semi-automatic, automatic and burst-fire modes, is particularly effective in urban settings, making it highly valuable to criminal groups engaged in territorial disputes.

Adding another layer to the threat, some gangs have acquired grenades and rocket-propelled grenade (RPG) launchers, further escalating the firepower accessible to them. While still relatively rare, incidents involving explosives have occurred in Sweden, where hand grenades often sourced from the Balkans have been used in gang-related violence and intimidation tactics. An RPG in criminal hands is an unsettling reality; its destructive potential not only threatens law enforcement personnel but also poses severe risks to civilians caught in the crossfire.

This influx of military-grade firearms and equipment is reshaping the criminal landscape and pushing law enforcement capabilities to their limits. With access to high-powered rifles, modified pistols, and even military-style carbines, these criminal groups have evolved into heavily armed entities, necessitating specialised police response teams. Traditional approaches to policing and public safety are simply inadequate in the face of adversaries with such lethal firepower. This shift signifies not merely an escalation in criminal armament but a transformation in how violence is carried out, with a level of weaponry that fundamentally alters the dynamics between law enforcement and organised crime.

Case Studies in Police Encounters

Consider a few specific incidents in which police forces encountered criminals wielding military-grade firearms, where the reality of facing off against weapons designed for battlefields underscored the shifting dynamics of criminal firepower. In the United States, the San Bernardino, California incident stands as a stark example. Here, in 2015, local police responded to a terrorist attack perpetrated by individuals carrying AR-15-style rifles, semi-automatic weapons designed to be highly customisable, allowing for the addition of larger magazines, scopes, and tactical grips that enhance control and firing accuracy. The attackers' rifles, equipped with 5.56mm ammunition standard in military contexts were devastating in their ability to penetrate walls and vehicles, creating hazards for law enforcement officers and civilians alike. Tactical units, including SWAT, were called in, transforming what began as a police response into a scene akin to a military operation, with armoured vehicles deployed to counteract the attackers' superior firepower.

A similar incident unfolded in 1997 in North Hollywood, Los Angeles, where police encountered two armed assailants in what became one of the most infamous gun battles in American history. The suspects were armed with Norinco Type 56 assault rifles Chinese-made variants of the AK-47 modified for fully automatic firing. Equipped with armour-piercing rounds, these firearms rendered the officers' standard-issue 9mm sidearms almost useless, as the bullets bounced off the suspects' body armour. For over 40 minutes, police were pinned down, and severely outgunned, until officers were forced to borrow AR-15 rifles from a nearby gun shop, an extraordinary measure underscoring their sheer lack of resources against such weaponry. The entire standoff was a harrowing demonstration of how inadequately prepared local police forces were to contend with adversaries carrying military-grade arms.

In Europe, too, incidents involving high-powered firearms have become a tragic reality. In 2015, during the Bataclan theatre attack in Paris, police confronted attackers wielding Zastava M70 rifles Yugoslavian variants of the AK-47, known for their durability and capacity to fire rapidly and consistently under adverse conditions. These rifles, sourced from Eastern European black markets, were capable of unleashing 7.62mm rounds with lethal accuracy, creating a nightmarish scenario for responding officers. The Bataclan incident highlighted how military-grade weaponry, particularly AK variants and other automatic rifles trafficked into Europe, poses a profound threat to urban safety and law enforcement capabilities.

In the UK, where firearms are far more restricted, instances of military-style weapons emerging are rare but all the more shocking when they do occur. In 2020, a police raid in Birmingham uncovered a cache of weapons including an Uzi submachine gun, an Israeli-designed firearm capable of firing 600 rounds per minute. This weapon, compact and favoured for its portability, has found popularity in criminal circles for its rapid rate of fire and lethal efficiency in close-quarters engagements. The discovery underscored the uncomfortable reality that even Britain's stringent gun laws cannot entirely prevent sophisticated firearms from reaching the hands of organised criminals.

In each of these incidents, the criminal possession of military-grade firearms transformed what should have been police engagements into outright battles, forcing law enforcement to adopt military-style tactics, gear, and support. From AR-15s to AK-47s and Uzis, these weapons underscore a distressing trend: as the firepower of criminal groups grows increasingly sophisticated, traditional policing methods struggle to keep pace, often leaving communities vulnerable and officers under-resourced in their duty to protect and serve.

Across the Atlantic, police in Belgium have found themselves confronting an alarming array of military-grade firearms wielded by organised crime groups, especially in cities like Antwerp, which has emerged as a central node for cocaine trafficking across Europe. In recent years, Antwerp has witnessed an escalating arms race within its criminal underworld, with weapons far beyond the capability of conventional law enforcement becoming commonplace. In a recent raid, Belgian police seized an arsenal that included FN SCAR rifles, a military-grade firearm manufactured domestically by FN Herstal and favoured by NATO forces for its accuracy, durability, and ability to handle high-calibre rounds. These SCAR rifles designed to deliver precise fire with devastating impact highlight the unsettling truth that transnational crime syndicates are acquiring military-grade arms with relative ease.

The raid in Antwerp also revealed a stockpile of Heckler & Koch MP5 submachine guns, another weapon of choice for military and specialised police forces worldwide. Compact yet powerful, the MP5 can fire up to 800 rounds per minute, making it highly effective in close quarters a favoured environment for criminal operations. The MP5's design allows for rapid-fire control, creating an intense threat in confined spaces such as city streets, where police find themselves drastically outgunned. Criminal groups use such weapons to enforce territorial dominance and protect drug routes, leaving local law enforcement increasingly cautious in their approach, given the sheer destructive power these firearms confer on those wielding them.

Even more concerning, the raid uncovered several M82 Barrett .50-calibre sniper rifles. These rifles, designed for extreme long-range accuracy and capable of penetrating armoured vehicles, are rarely seen outside military and specialised anti-terror units. In criminal hands, such a weapon has a chilling capability: it can neutralise targets from a kilometre away, effectively creating a "no-go zone" for police. Belgian authorities were deeply troubled by the discovery, as the presence of such sniper rifles implies a level of strategic planning and resource allocation within these criminal networks that verges on paramilitary.

The disparity between the equipment available to law enforcement and that accessible to criminals has left parts of cities like Antwerp near lawless. For example, criminal factions with access to the aforementioned SCAR rifles and Barrett sniper rifles create de facto strongholds, fortified zones where police presence is minimal and cautiously controlled. Officers entering these neighbourhoods risk ambushes from criminals whose firepower not only surpasses the police's standard-issue equipment but renders armoured vehicles vulnerable. Without equivalent armament or tactical capabilities, local police forces must navigate these areas with extreme caution, knowing that they face combatants equipped with weapons engineered to withstand military engagements.

This growing militarisation within organised crime reflects a troubling trend: these weapons are not merely tools but symbols of power and intimidation, altering the balance in the constant struggle between law enforcement and crime syndicates. Transnational crime syndicates, bolstered by an arms network that connects black markets across Europe, have turned parts of Antwerp and other cities into fortified hubs for their operations. It has become apparent that traditional policing strategies are inadequate in the face of such military-grade firepower, as these groups embed themselves within communities, effectively carving out zones of impunity.

The Role of Black-Market Supply Chains

The distribution of military-grade firearms into criminal networks operates along a labyrinthine series of black-market supply chains, closely intertwined with the trafficking routes for drugs like fentanyl and the smuggling of human beings. These are not merely routes but established, well-oiled systems, spanning continents and exploiting regions where governance is weak, borders are permeable, and corruption can be counted upon. In essence, the trafficking of arms is part of a vast network of illicit trade, capitalising on the very same pathways that facilitate the transport of fentanyl and human trafficking victims across borders.

In the United States, the southern border remains a major entry point for these weapons. High-powered firearms often originate from countries like Mexico and Guatemala, where long-standing conflicts have left behind caches of military-grade rifles and automatic weapons. These arms are moved north through Central American smuggling channels before they reach the US-Mexico border. Here, drug cartels, deeply entrenched in the trafficking of both narcotics and human beings, have perfected the methods of circumventing border security, allowing firearms to slip across alongside their other illicit goods. Once inside, these weapons are distributed to local gangs and criminal groups, often through networks tightly bound by cartel influence, reaching American cities where they fuel gang violence and drug-related turf wars.

In Europe, the challenges are equally severe but follow a different geography. With the Schengen Agreement allowing relatively open movement between European countries, traffickers have the advantage of bypassing stringent border checks once they enter the EU. Much of the firearms supply comes from Eastern Europe, where decades of armed conflict particularly in the Balkans left a surplus of weapons now funnelling into Western Europe. Eastern European countries like Serbia, Croatia, and Bulgaria are key source points, where arms once produced for regional militaries and warlords are sold off to brokers and intermediaries. From there, the weapons flow through countries with weak border enforcement and corruptible customs officials, reaching the likes of France, Germany, and Belgium, where criminal syndicates readily incorporate these firearms into their arsenals.

The weapons themselves range from AK-47s and Kalashnikovs iconic and durable assault rifles that originated from Soviet-era production lines to newer, equally lethal models like the Zastava M70 and Vz. 58 rifles, produced in Eastern Europe. The traffickers transporting these weapons operate within a larger black market apparatus, heavily interconnected with narcotics and human smuggling networks. It's not uncommon for a single smuggling route to carry a combination of guns, drugs, and human trafficking victims, maximising profits by transporting multiple illicit "commodities" at once. These criminal organisations exploit the desperate human flow of migrants, particularly at vulnerable entry points like the US-Mexico border or the Mediterranean crossing into southern Europe, to mask their activities and evade detection.

The Mediterranean, in particular, has become a notorious conduit for illegal firearms into Europe. As waves of migrants attempt to cross from North Africa and the Middle East, often escaping war zones, smugglers use these desperate flows as cover, moving weapons alongside human cargo. Guns are often transported from conflict-ridden areas like Libya or Syria, where the proliferation of firearms has created a ready supply for illicit arms dealers. Traffickers utilise smuggling routes through Tunisia, Libya, and Egypt, and from there, boats carrying migrants and weapons set sail for southern European coasts. Italian authorities, especially in Sicily, have increasingly intercepted vessels that mix firearms with drugs and trafficked individuals a vivid example of the brazen opportunism of these criminal networks.

Efforts by governments to clamp down on this trade face substantial obstacles, not least due to the scale of corruption within customs and border enforcement agencies. In many cases, criminal networks have developed sophisticated bribery schemes to ensure safe passage. Customs officials along key transit routes in Eastern Europe and Central America can be incentivised to look the other way, allowing container loads of arms to slip through ports and checkpoints with minimal scrutiny. For instance, the Antwerp port, Europe's second-largest, has been identified as a frequent entry point for smuggled firearms, as well as a distribution hub for drugs like cocaine. Traffickers exploit the high volume of legitimate goods passing through to disguise arms shipments among otherwise innocuous cargo.

The black market for military-grade weapons, therefore, operates as an almost parallel supply chain to the global trade in fentanyl and the illicit movement of human beings. It is as organised as any legal enterprise, complete with designated transport networks, trusted suppliers, and specific routes that allow high-powered firearms to end up in the hands of criminal syndicates operating in Western cities. Moreover, with no adherence to the civilian restrictions that define legal firearm ownership, this black market renders gun control efforts largely ineffective. The very laws intended to protect citizens instead create a vacuum filled by these criminal enterprises, supplying an arsenal of weapons that are outright banned from civilian use, ensuring that criminal groups remain well-armed and a step ahead of conventional law enforcement. This convergence of arms, drugs, and human trafficking presents a uniquely dangerous challenge, one that can only be addressed by acknowledging the transnational reach and multi-faceted nature of these black-market empires.

The Impact on Law Enforcement and Public Safety

The infiltration of military-grade firearms into the hands of criminal organisations has indeed created an untenable situation for law enforcement. When local police officers, many of whom are equipped only with standard-issue pistols or low-calibre firearms, are forced to confront criminals wielding high-powered assault rifles, semi-automatics, and sometimes even explosives, the balance shifts drastically. In towns and smaller cities where budgets do not allow for the same level of tactical equipment or training afforded to metropolitan police forces, officers find themselves at a striking disadvantage. It's an imbalance that effectively hampers police response and, ultimately, jeopardises public safety.

This disparity has emboldened criminal organisations in ways we might never have anticipated. Knowing they have the upper hand, these groups have grown more audacious, carrying out violent acts with a confidence born not from skill alone, but from a sense of superiority in firepower. Consider, for example, a police force in a modest town, tasked with addressing a gang dispute involving military-grade weaponry. These officers, reliant on traditional firearms and possibly outdated body armour, face adversaries who can discharge dozens of high-velocity rounds in seconds with firearms with the capacity to penetrate standard police vests, vehicles, and barriers. In essence, such confrontations push local law enforcement into a position where tactical retreat may be their only viable option, leaving communities under siege.

The presence of these high-calibre weapons doesn't merely change the scale of violence; it transforms the nature of criminal activity itself. Armed with military-grade weapons, criminals can operate with impunity, often choosing to engage in prolonged shootouts rather than flee, confident that police forces will lack the firepower or reinforcements to subdue them. This dynamic was seen in one particularly harrowing incident in the suburbs of Paris, where a gang dispute erupted into open warfare on the streets, with criminals openly brandishing Kalashnikovs and other automatic rifles. Police arriving at the scene were immediately outmatched, unable to intervene effectively without risking serious harm to themselves and civilians caught in the crossfire.

In urban centres, too, this escalation has transformed otherwise "standard" criminal activity into deadly encounters. Armed robberies, for instance, are no longer brief operations to steal and escape quickly; now, criminals are equipped for extended standoffs with police if needed. There have been numerous incidents where, armed with automatic weapons, criminals not only outgunned the police but could position themselves tactically, taking advantage of high-capacity magazines that allow them to sustain a barrage of fire. In some cases, they use modified assault rifles, capable of both rapid-fire and precision targeting, making them a danger not only to law enforcement but also to anyone who happens to be within range.

Gang-related conflicts, too, have become far more lethal with the influx of such weaponry. The violent disputes between criminal groups are no longer just over territorial control or "business" turf but have evolved into displays of dominance through firepower. In cities across Europe and North America, these conflicts have seen a disturbing rise in casualties, often involving innocent bystanders. A case in Chicago exemplifies this tragic reality; a feud between rival gangs turned a neighbourhood into a virtual war zone. Heavily armed members clashed with such intensity that residents were forced to take cover in their own homes, with police reluctant to intervene without backup or special units. The level of firepower wielded by these gangs was far beyond the capacity of standard police patrols to handle.

The ripple effects of this militarisation of criminal arsenals extend to the public, with civilians increasingly caught in the crossfire. Incidents of stray bullets claiming the lives of innocent bystanders are rising alarmingly. With high-powered firearms in criminal hands, a gang dispute or an armed robbery quickly escalates to a lethal threat to anyone nearby. Automatic weapons, by design, are built to spray rounds over a wide area, making it almost impossible to control the damage done to those within proximity. The indiscriminate nature of these shootings leaves civilians not only physically endangered but psychologically scarred, instilling a pervasive sense of fear and insecurity in their communities.

Moreover, this surge in military-grade weaponry has bred a culture of intimidation among criminal groups. Knowing that they possess superior firepower, criminals use these weapons as a means of instilling fear, not just in rival groups but in the general public. By brandishing these firearms, criminals create an environment where citizens feel increasingly vulnerable and, in many cases, begin to distrust the ability of law enforcement to protect them. In some neighbourhoods, gangs have used their weapons to "claim" areas, creating no-go zones where residents are hesitant to call the police for fear of reprisal.

These dynamics signify a breakdown in civil security. When criminals wield such firepower and know that law enforcement is outmatched, we risk normalising a situation where communities feel permanently under siege, and police forces are continually on the defensive. As police are forced into tactical compromises to avoid confrontation, this breeds an environment where crime becomes more entrenched, where law enforcement's deterrent effect is diluted, and where public safety suffers immensely. It's a cycle that, left unchecked, threatens to deepen the divide between communities and the institutions meant to protect them.

Laws Aimed at Civilian Access and Their Unintended Consequences

Ironically, the very laws designed to protect citizens by restricting access to firearms have, in many cases, accomplished the opposite. In countries like the UK, where the government enforces strict gun control policies, the intention is to reduce gun violence by limiting access to weapons altogether. These policies stem from a belief that, by removing firearms from the general populace, incidents of gun violence will naturally decrease. However, this approach presumes a level playing field where criminals are equally constrained by law, and where state resources are sufficient to respond rapidly and effectively to threats. Unfortunately, this is not the reality.

Law-abiding citizens in the UK are prohibited from owning firearms for self-defence, with restrictions so stringent that even obtaining a permit for a basic handgun is next to impossible. Weapons of any kind, particularly firearms, are seen by the government as best left in the hands of the police or military, based on the principle that public safety is a collective responsibility managed by state forces. However, the government's guarantee of protection does not always translate into timely action, especially in rural areas or during escalating violent incidents in urban settings. Citizens are ultimately left in a position where they must rely entirely on a response system that is often overstretched and, in some cases, unable to provide the swift protection needed in emergencies.

This vacuum, created by restrictive laws, does little to deter those operating outside the legal framework. Criminals have no qualms about circumventing legislation, sourcing military-grade weaponry through black market channels, often facilitated by transnational crime syndicates or loosely regulated borders within Europe. These illicit networks ensure that criminals have access to firearms far beyond what is available to the average citizen or even, in many cases, to the local police. In recent years, weapons trafficked from the Balkans or regions of instability in Eastern Europe have made their way into the hands of organised crime groups across the UK, from gangland territories in London to the once-quiet streets of smaller towns. This influx of firepower has escalated the level of violence in criminal disputes, where armed groups feel emboldened knowing that the average citizen has little means of defending themselves.

For law-abiding citizens, the prohibition on firearms isn't just a denial of access to weapons; it is a denial of agency in their defence. They face the realisation that, should they encounter a violent situation, they must depend entirely on the arrival of police a service that, due to budget constraints, understaffing, or sheer geographic spread, may not be able to respond as swiftly as needed. The disempowerment of citizens through these policies can foster a sense of helplessness, particularly as instances of violent crime involving firearms make headline news. It is a bitter irony: while criminals arm themselves with relative ease, the law-abiding public is restricted by measures that, though intended to enhance safety, leave them more vulnerable.

Across the Atlantic, we see a different scenario. In the United States, despite ongoing debates around gun control, citizens have the constitutional right to bear arms. Yet, even in cities with some of the strictest gun laws, like Chicago, rampant gun violence persists due to the flow of illegal weapons. The city's prohibitive laws, intended to curb violence, have not stemmed the tide of firearms pouring in from other states with looser restrictions or from illegal sources, leaving law-abiding residents caught in the crossfire. This situation underscores the limitations of regulation that fails to address the deeper issue: the unchecked movement of firearms via black market networks, which are neither hindered by local legislation nor respectful of borders.

These examples highlight a fundamental paradox within the gun control debate: restrictive policies intended to create safer societies by limiting firearm access for all citizens, rather than targeting the sources of illicit weaponry, often miss the mark. Rather than stemming violence, these measures risk leaving ordinary people defenceless in the face of well-armed criminals, who operate with near impunity thanks to underground supply chains. Without addressing the transnational nature of gun trafficking, or the pervasive reach of organised crime, such restrictions can end up emboldening those who operate outside the law while diminishing the rights and the safety of those within it.

Case Studies: The US and Europe

To truly grasp the scale and gravity of these issues, we must look at concrete cases from both the United States and Europe, where the flow of military-grade firearms into criminal hands has become alarmingly routine. In cities like Los Angeles, for example, law enforcement officials are facing a seemingly insurmountable task: dismantling cartel-linked gangs that are increasingly armed with automatic weapons, such as AK-47s, AR-15s, and high-calibre sniper rifles. This firepower is not typically intended for local disputes but rather for holding and expanding control over drug-trafficking routes, where the ability to intimidate rivals or the police is a crucial advantage. These firearms largely originate from trafficking networks that cartels in Mexico have painstakingly constructed over the years, working through corrupt officials and using sophisticated smuggling tactics to transport weapons from south to north. Ironically, while much of the

US attention focuses on southbound drug trafficking, the northbound trafficking of firearms into America's cities is arming gangs and fuelling violence on its streets.

One particularly notable incident in Los Angeles involved the discovery of an entire cache of weapons in the hands of a cartel-affiliated gang. Police found an assortment of fully automatic rifles, shotguns, and even grenades all smuggled into the country via Mexican drug corridors. These weapons had been trafficked alongside shipments of narcotics, concealed within hidden compartments of vehicles, or even broken down into parts to avoid detection before reassembly on American soil. The power that these weapons provide, when combined with the organisational capabilities of cartel-backed gangs, has allowed these groups to establish fortified strongholds within certain city districts. Entire neighbourhoods become quasi-territories where gangs wield near-military strength, often overwhelming local police forces who are neither armed nor trained to handle such weaponry. As a result, response units must rely on specialised SWAT teams just to enter these areas safely a clear indication that conventional law enforcement strategies are inadequate against these well-armed, highly organised criminal groups.

Turning to Europe, a similar scenario plays out in cities like Stockholm, where gang violence has escalated dramatically, driven in large part by the ease of access to black-market weapons. Swedish police report an influx of arms from Balkan states, where leftover military stockpiles from the conflicts of the 1990s have flooded the black market, creating a readily available supply for organised crime syndicates operating across Europe. These firearms, often including assault rifles, machine guns, and even rocket-propelled grenades, are transported across borders with alarming ease, taking advantage of the Schengen Agreement's relaxed border controls. Once in Stockholm, these weapons empower criminal groups engaged in everything from drug trafficking to contract killings, with gang disputes frequently spilling into the public sphere. Shootouts and explosive attacks have become disturbingly frequent, with innocent bystanders at significant risk. The Swedish police have publicly stated that they are now dealing with "urban warfare" tactics previously unseen in civilian policing.

In Paris, we see another dimension of this issue. Here, the availability of military-grade weapons has fuelled conflicts within urban gangs as well as extremist groups operating within French borders. After a series of high-profile terrorist attacks, French authorities uncovered weaponry sourced from Eastern European black-market routes, often with a direct line to former Soviet bloc arsenals. Investigations revealed that these arms were transported into France by highly organised smuggling rings, using sophisticated techniques to bypass customs checks. From AK-47s to sniper rifles, these weapons have found their way into Parisian gangs, making their presence known in high-stakes heists and violent turf battles. With such weapons in their hands, gangs can challenge police with an audacity that would have been unthinkable a decade ago. The rise of these weapons has transformed some suburbs into virtual no-go zones, where police are reluctant to engage due to the overwhelming firepower of the criminal groups entrenched there.

These case studies highlight a deeply entrenched issue that transcends borders. Military-grade firearms are no longer anomalies in the criminal landscape of either the United States or Europe; they are part of a systemic crisis where transnational smuggling networks and local criminal groups operate in symbiosis. Cartel-affiliated gangs in Los Angeles and Stockholm's Balkan-armed syndicates share a common feature: they thrive on the availability of illicit military-grade weapons, enabling them to challenge state authority and expand their criminal enterprises with unprecedented force. As the demand for these weapons continues, the underground market only grows more robust, further embedding these firearms into the fabric of urban crime on both sides of the Atlantic. The result is a new, far more dangerous criminal landscape where law enforcement is consistently outgunned and the public is increasingly left exposed to the fallout of this unchecked arms race.

The Urgency of Addressing Illicit Weapon Flows

The surge of military-grade firearms in criminal networks has created a grim new reality for communities across the West, leaving citizens with a troubling question: are our governments genuinely doing what is necessary to tackle this problem, or are they simply clamping down on the legal civilian market while organised crime flourishes? As a citizen observing the current landscape, I see repeated crackdowns on legal gun owners individuals who go through rigorous background checks, licensing, and responsible ownership requirements while the criminal underworld seemingly accesses powerful weaponry with impunity. This imbalance between the actions taken against lawful civilians and those taken against well-armed criminals often appears ideologically driven or, at worst, a deflection due to the inability to target more dangerous networks.

Government responses have indeed been limited and, in many cases, misdirected. Western governments, for the most part, have focused heavily on strengthening domestic gun control laws, ostensibly to prevent firearms from falling into criminal hands. However, this approach primarily impacts legal gun owners and has had little effect on black-market trafficking. Efforts to enforce stricter gun control on civilians have led to an increased administrative burden on those who already comply with the law, yet these measures fail to address the real issue: the unregulated and international flow of military-grade weapons that fuel organised crime and terror groups.

The government's approach to tackling illicit arms trafficking has been largely fragmented and, in some cases, alarmingly passive. In Europe, for example, efforts to address the black-market influx of firearms from the Balkans and Eastern Europe remain hampered by weak border checks and the lack of comprehensive collaboration among EU member states. While there have been calls for stronger tracking systems and intelligence-sharing initiatives, these measures have been slow to materialise and insufficiently resourced. The Schengen Agreement, while invaluable for trade and travel, has also opened loopholes that traffickers exploit, moving weapons across borders with relative ease. When it comes to Eastern Europe, where arms are smuggled from former conflict zones into Western Europe, these routes are well-established, and traffickers have found reliable ways to bypass weakened border checks or use covert supply routes.

Across the Atlantic, the United States faces its own set of challenges. Rather than fully addressing the northbound flow of military-grade firearms from Latin America a direct consequence of cartel and gang activity in Mexico the government has prioritised restricting civilian gun ownership through laws targeting high-capacity magazines, semi-automatic rifles, and other such features. Yet the cartels remain largely unaffected by these domestic restrictions. Cartels have developed smuggling routes and sophisticated logistical operations to traffic firearms alongside drugs, using tunnels, bribery, and false documentation to bypass detection. Despite the bipartisan acknowledgement of these issues, actions have largely been confined to periodic crackdowns and one-off operations rather than establishing a sustained, tactical effort to combat these cartels' influence and their northbound weapon trafficking.

Internationally, collaboration on combating arms trafficking remains minimal, particularly when compared to other global issues. While there are some international agreements, such as the United Nations Arms Trade Treaty, the enforcement and scope of these treaties are often limited, and there is little evidence of real impact in curbing the availability of military-grade firearms to organised crime. The treaty primarily focuses on state-to-state weapons transfers, often missing the more covert black-market channels used by criminals. Where arms control laws attempt to restrict the import and export of weapons, they inadvertently raise the value of these firearms on the black market, making it an even more lucrative trade for those willing to take the risks. The irony, therefore, is that restrictions meant to curb firearm distribution may unintentionally incentivise illegal sales, as restricted items become more desirable commodities.

For citizens, the lack of effective action to disrupt this black-market trade leaves us vulnerable. Criminals face few real obstacles in acquiring highly dangerous weapons, while law-abiding citizens are increasingly stripped of their means to defend themselves. Law enforcement, too, suffers from this imbalance. Even as they are outgunned on the streets, officers face political and bureaucratic limitations, with budgets that may not allow for adequate training or equipment. In cases where special tactical units are deployed, response times may be significantly delayed, which hardly serves as a reliable measure for everyday public safety. The frustration among police forces in both the United States and Europe is palpable; many officers understand the grave risks posed by these weapons but are constrained by a system that prioritises regulation over realistic, on-the-ground measures against illegal trafficking.

What is required, then, is a comprehensive shift in strategy one that prioritises dismantling the infrastructure of arms trafficking and focuses on international collaboration rather than merely burdening legal owners. Western governments need to invest in intelligence-led policing, increase funding for specialised units, and establish dedicated task forces to track, intercept, and dismantle arms trafficking routes. Internationally, they must develop stronger alliances and share intelligence more freely to disrupt the flow of weapons before they reach our borders. These are difficult tasks, requiring both political will and significant financial commitment, but they are essential if we are to address the issue of military-grade firearms and ensure that law enforcement and by extension, the public are no longer outmatched.

Until such comprehensive measures are adopted, we remain at risk, caught between governments focused on restricting civilian ownership and criminal syndicates that face no such limitations in arming themselves with the deadliest firearms. The result is a weakened social contract: one in which citizens are expected to rely on law enforcement for protection, yet see that enforcement is consistently outgunned by the very criminals it seeks to contain. Without a true shift in focus, governments risk further undermining public confidence in their capacity to provide safety, leaving citizens in a precarious position that legislation alone cannot resolve.

Chapter 7: Comparative Case Studies: Gun Control in the USA, Europe, and the UK

The landscape of gun control in the Western world offers a fascinating study in contrasts, particularly when examining the approaches of the United States, Europe, and the United Kingdom. Each region's policies are underpinned by distinct historical and cultural influences, legal structures, and philosophical beliefs about the right to self-defence, public safety, and government control. Through a comparative lens, this chapter will explore the outcomes of these policies, analysing both crime statistics and personal accounts to evaluate the effectiveness of restrictive laws. The central question is simple yet profound: Have these measures succeeded in reducing violent crime, or have they inadvertently exacerbated it?

In the United States, the right to bear arms is enshrined in the Second Amendment a protection so fundamental that it has become integral to the national identity. Yet the outcomes are complex. In Europe, where restrictive gun laws prevail, we see similarly complex results. The UK, with one of the strictest regimes, has an almost total prohibition of civilian firearm ownership, and while firearm-related homicides are rare, knife crime and unarmed violent attacks are on the rise. It is clear that each approach yields a different profile of violence, but what remains common is a troubling failure to eliminate crime. The reality is that in many of these cases, laws aimed at restricting firearm access for law-abiding citizens have failed to curb crime effectively and, in some instances, have even contributed to increases in unarmed or gang-related violence.

USA: The Paradox of Armed Rights and Violent Crime

In the United States, the constitutional right to own firearms is as fiercely protected as it is contested. The Second Amendment, drafted during an era when the very notion of freedom and self-governance was newly forged, guaranteed the right to bear arms not simply as a safeguard against individual crime but as a bulwark against tyranny. This foundational right has, however, become deeply entangled with the modern epidemic of gun violence, the prevalence of mass shootings, and the ever-expanding black market for illegal firearms particularly in major cities with some of the country's most restrictive gun control laws, like Chicago and Los Angeles.

For all the energy poured into crafting new firearm regulations, it appears that government efforts to target criminal networks and intercept illegal firearms at their source fall short. Federal and local agencies certainly undertake programmes aimed at curbing gun violence initiatives like the federal Bureau of Alcohol, Tobacco, Firearms, and Explosives (ATF) tracing and tracking operations, or the controversial "red flag" laws that permit law enforcement to confiscate firearms from individuals deemed to be a risk. Yet, these efforts appear narrowly focused on legal loopholes and civilian gun ownership rather than directly addressing the criminal trafficking networks that persist and, by many accounts, expand. This seeming focus on the easier-to-police civilian market leaves the organised crime networks the true engines of gun trafficking largely untouched.

Part of the problem is bureaucratic and political. Tackling gun violence at the criminal level requires inter-agency cooperation, funding for specific task forces, and often international cooperation, as many firearms flow into the United States from foreign black-market networks. Some measures, like the Department of Justice's Project Safe Neighborhoods (PSN), do try to address violent crime by working with local law enforcement to identify and prosecute "the most violent offenders." However, such programmes often suffer from inconsistent application, regional disparities, and a focus on reactive measures rather than proactive intelligence gathering on trafficking networks. Furthermore, these efforts are dwarfed by the emphasis placed on symbolic measures like buyback programmes, often touted by officials as effective despite their limited impact on the criminal underworld, which does not rely on legal or registered firearms.

Cities like Chicago have tried to combat gun violence with extensive gun restrictions, only to find themselves with higher rates of gun crime, much of it committed with illegal weapons trafficked from neighbouring states with less stringent gun laws. This city-to-city inconsistency in regulation due to America's patchwork of state laws means that even the most restrictive policies are ultimately limited by their scope. Criminal organisations and traffickers know how to exploit these gaps, moving firearms across state lines with relative ease. Meanwhile, states with fewer restrictions, like Texas and New Hampshire, see lower rates of violent crime, partly because of the deterrent effect of an armed populace, but also due to a stronger tradition of lawful gun ownership and a less ideologically charged approach to policing and enforcement.

One glaring issue is the ideological framing of gun control in the political sphere, which often constrains substantive action against criminal gun violence. In the current climate, government policy on firearms is deeply polarised, with ideological commitments frequently overtaking practical crime-fighting considerations. Many politicians and officials argue that the solution lies in further restricting legal gun ownership rather than addressing the enforcement failures and limitations in tackling the black market directly. By framing the issue as a matter of civilian responsibility, they sidestep the more complicated, resource-intensive issue of interdicting the black market flow of guns to criminal groups.

Further complicating the picture is the impact of the "defund the police" movement and similar policy shifts, which have diminished resources for law enforcement in several major cities. This reduction in funding hinders the very departments responsible for tracking and targeting criminal gun markets, creating a situation where crime prevention is undermined by the diversion of resources away from tactical and investigative units and into bureaucratic or social service initiatives. While these alternative approaches have merit in addressing root causes of crime, they are no substitute for direct criminal enforcement when it comes to firearms trafficking.

Ultimately, the government's current stance on gun violence appears to be more focused on politically visible actions such as tightening civilian gun regulations than on confronting the underground gun market. Initiatives to curb legal ownership may garner public approval and align with certain ideological stances, but they largely ignore the reality that criminals are not acquiring their firearms from legal vendors. As a result, law-abiding citizens face increased restrictions on their right to self-defence, while criminal organisations continue to operate unabated, facilitated by weak borders, insufficiently funded enforcement agencies, and policies that focus on optics rather than effectiveness.

For a solution that genuinely addresses the heart of gun violence, Western governments, particularly in the United States, would need to pivot away from the civilian market crackdown and tackle the structural and cross-border dimensions of gun trafficking. This would involve bolstering ATF capabilities, improving intelligence-sharing between federal and state agencies, and strengthening partnerships with international counterparts to disrupt smuggling routes. Without such a pivot, it seems we are left with a troubling paradox: an abundance of restrictive gun laws that do little to deter criminals while disproportionately burdening law-abiding citizens. As a concerned citizen, it is hard not to feel that the government's energies are misdirected and focused on ideological battles over civilian ownership rather than the more arduous but essential task of dismantling the criminal networks that drive gun violence in the first place.

Europe: Restrictive Measures, Diverse Outcomes

Europe presents a markedly different model of gun control from the United States. Countries like France, Germany, and the UK have enacted strict regulations that make legal firearm ownership extremely difficult for ordinary citizens, with comprehensive background checks, mandatory training, and psychological evaluations. Germany's stringent requirements, for instance, necessitate proof of "need," safe storage, and a waiting period, making firearms nearly inaccessible to those without a compelling reason. France has similar hurdles, mandating medical clearance, clean criminal records, and official permits, which restrict firearm access to highly specific categories of citizens, such as sport shooters and hunters. The aim is clear: to minimise gun violence through comprehensive restrictions on civilian ownership. But as any observer of European crime trends can see, such measures do not necessarily translate to a safer society, especially when it comes to organised crime and terrorism.

In Germany, the illusion of robust public safety was shattered in 2019 when a gunman targeted a synagogue in Halle, an attack that revealed uncomfortable gaps in Germany's strict regulatory framework. The perpetrator had circumvented strict firearms controls through crude but effective workarounds, constructing his weapons and using online resources to bypass regulations entirely. This incident was a stark reminder that determined individuals will often find a way around even the most exhaustive legal barriers. More disturbingly, it highlighted a fundamental flaw in the system: strict gun laws seem effective at limiting access for law-abiding citizens but do little to address the underlying security vulnerabilities exploited by determined criminals.

France, too, faces a similar predicament. Despite one of Europe's strictest gun policies, with limited categories of civilian ownership and rigorous police vetting, the nation has been rocked by violent incidents involving firearms. In recent years, Paris has witnessed several deadly terrorist attacks carried out with military-grade weapons, including assault rifles and grenades firearms well outside the reach of legal civilian markets. These weapons typically enter France through smuggling routes, flowing in from Eastern Europe and the Balkans, where conflicts have left behind an abundance of firearms. Criminal syndicates and terrorist networks exploit these black-market channels, supplying weapons that the civilian population could never legally access but that still end up on the streets of Europe's major cities.

The problem, in part, stems from Europe's open-border policies under the Schengen Agreement. While this agreement has undeniably facilitated easier movement for law-abiding citizens and promoted trade and tourism, it has also unintentionally aided the movement of illicit arms. With minimal internal border checks, smuggling routes between Eastern and Western Europe have flourished. Organised crime groups, already adept at trafficking drugs and human beings, now capitalise on these same routes to transport firearms. In France, for instance, authorities have intercepted smuggled weapons originating from Bosnia and Herzegovina, an area awash with weapons since the 1990s conflicts. Criminal groups in cities like Marseille and Paris rely on these channels, allowing a thriving black market to operate despite strict domestic gun laws.

So, what are European governments doing to combat this influx of black-market firearms? The answer is, unfortunately, fragmented and often insufficient. France has initiated several high-profile anti-trafficking operations in collaboration with Europol and other EU member states. Operation Bosphorus, for instance, sought to disrupt smuggling routes from the Balkans, and while it had some success in capturing firearms and arresting traffickers, the sheer scale of the issue has made such operations piecemeal at best. Germany, too, has joined EU-wide initiatives, including the European Multidisciplinary Platform Against Criminal Threats (EMPACT), which targets organised crime networks across the continent. But even with these collaborative measures, illicit arms continue to flow.

Part of the challenge lies in European governance itself. While Europe has cooperative mechanisms through agencies like Europol, it lacks the centralised enforcement capacity of a single state such as the USA. Each EU member state enforces its laws, and differences in legal frameworks create inconsistencies in enforcement. For instance, what qualifies as an illegal firearm in one nation may not be treated the same way in another. This patchwork of laws enables traffickers to exploit the weakest links, transporting firearms through countries with more lenient laws before distributing them to higher-demand markets in Western Europe.

France and Germany have also turned to surveillance and intelligence-sharing as preventative measures, but these approaches do little to tackle the broader structural issue. Smuggling routes are well-established, and black-market sellers are highly adept at concealing their networks, utilising encrypted messaging platforms, the dark web, and sophisticated money-laundering techniques. Despite Europe's technological and financial resources, cracking down on such networks has proven far more difficult than restricting civilian gun ownership.

As a citizen observing these trends, it's hard to ignore the ideological undertones that influence the approach to gun control in Europe. Rather than acknowledging the pervasive black market and re-evaluating border policies or enforcement strategies, authorities focus primarily on limiting civilian access. This policy orientation aligns with broader European values of demilitarisation and public safety, yet it overlooks the grim reality that criminal elements are unimpeded by legal restrictions. Organised crime syndicates continue to access firearms with relative ease, while ordinary citizens face near-insurmountable barriers should they wish to own a firearm for self-defence.

If European governments are serious about addressing gun violence, they would need to broaden their focus beyond civilian ownership to a coordinated, transnational approach to curbing black-market firearms. This would entail tightening border controls within the Schengen Zone, increasing funding for anti-trafficking intelligence operations, and empowering EU-wide enforcement bodies like Europol to play a more active role in tackling arms trafficking networks. However, such measures remain largely absent from the public discourse, with authorities seeming more inclined to target the "visible" issue of civilian gun ownership than the far more complex, and politically sensitive, problem of transnational smuggling.

For now, Europe's gun control policies appear to accomplish one thing effectively: keeping firearms out of the hands of law-abiding citizens while leaving the black-market trade largely undisturbed. It's a paradox that reveals the limitations of ideology-driven policymaking in the face of an increasingly complex criminal landscape. As a concerned citizen, I can only wonder whether European leaders will ever shift their focus from restricting civilian freedoms to dismantling the criminal networks that continue to threaten public safety across the continent.

The UK: Total Prohibition and Its Consequences

The United Kingdom's approach to gun control is undoubtedly one of the most restrictive frameworks in the Western world, a status it achieved largely in response to the tragic events of the 1996 Dunblane massacre. Following the massacre, public and political sentiment converged swiftly, and Parliament enacted the Firearms (Amendment) Act 1997, which outlawed almost all civilian ownership of handguns and significantly tightened controls on rifles and shotguns. Today, only licensed individuals, typically farmers or sport shooters, are permitted to own certain types of long guns, and even these are regulated with exacting scrutiny. Acquiring a firearm legally is a rigorous process involving background checks, home visits, mental health evaluations, and the approval of two references. As a result, incidents of gun violence are indeed rare. Yet, I would argue that this stringent control on civilian ownership has not wholly prevented violence; rather, it has merely shifted the form that violent crime takes in the UK.

Knife crime has become a defining issue in recent years, with the UK now experiencing a disturbing rise in knife-related violence, especially among youth. The statistics are troubling. The Office for National Statistics (ONS) reports that knife-related offences have been climbing steadily, with London and Manchester witnessing some of the highest rates. Youth gangs, operating in areas plagued by socio-economic challenges, often view knife possession as essential for protection, status, or intimidation. The Metropolitan Police has recorded knife offences doubling in the past decade alone. Some neighbourhoods are now more familiar with the sight of makeshift memorials for young victims of knife violence than they are with police patrols.

While knife crime dominates headlines, this isn't the only form of violence we're grappling with. Acid attacks, too, have emerged as a shockingly common form of assault. Once rare, acid attacks in the UK now rank among the highest per capita in the world, with victims often left disfigured and traumatised. The UK's strict gun control laws may have curtailed gun violence among the general populace, but they have done little to curb other violent crimes, leaving citizens acutely vulnerable to these alternative threats. I can't help but feel that this focus on gun control has somewhat blinded our government to the broader issue of violence itself.

Moreover, the myth that gun crimes are nonexistent in the UK is simply not true. While gun-related incidents are fewer than in the US or even parts of mainland Europe, they still exist, and they are almost always linked to organised crime networks. British gangs continue to acquire firearms through black-market channels. For example, firearms from Eastern Europe are smuggled into the UK, often crossing porous borders within the European Union before reaching British shores. The "County Lines" drug networks, which operate on a vast scale, also rely on firearms to enforce territory and control. The UK Border Force does intercept a number of these weapons each year, but this is a fraction of what likely slips through undetected.

Interestingly, the types of firearms recovered in UK black-market seizures are far from rudimentary. In recent years, law enforcement agencies have noted an increase in the presence of military-grade firearms, including automatic rifles and even grenades, which have been trafficked from conflict zones in the Balkans and beyond. Some of these weapons are reactivated decommissioned firearms, a trade that has proven alarmingly resilient. Just last year, police discovered a gun factory in Sussex where firearms were being reactivated and sold to organised crime groups across the country. This discovery only underscored a frustrating paradox: despite near-total prohibition for law-abiding citizens, those intent on violent criminals, gang members, and even potential terrorists appear unfazed by these restrictions. The underground trade in firearms not only persists but thrives.

Yet, what are Western governments, particularly the UK, truly doing to address this issue? There are initiatives, to be sure, but they seem disjointed and, to my mind, rather superficial. The UK government has introduced measures like the Offensive Weapons Act, which targets knives and corrosive substances. The police have ramped up stop-and-search efforts, albeit controversially, with significant public resistance and accusations of discriminatory practices. Youth intervention programmes have received some additional funding, with community initiatives aimed at diverting young people away from gang involvement. These are all worthwhile endeavours, but they feel inadequate against the scale of the problem.

A far more coordinated response is needed if we are to effectively combat the black-market arms trade. The National Crime Agency (NCA), the UK's equivalent of the FBI, works with Europol and other European agencies to track firearms trafficking, but its resources are stretched. The NCA's mandate covers a vast range of criminal activities, from human trafficking to drug smuggling, and as a result, firearms trafficking receives relatively little of the agency's limited manpower and funding. Our intelligence efforts are further hampered by post-Brexit limitations on cooperation with European partners, complicating efforts to monitor and intercept weapons smuggled from the Continent.

Ironically, it appears that while the UK government remains committed to curtailing civilian access to firearms, it has not demonstrated the same resolve in tackling the criminal networks responsible for trafficking them. A stricter crackdown on known trafficking routes, backed by intelligence-led policing and increased international cooperation, would make a far greater impact on violent crime than additional restrictions on law-abiding citizens. Yet, this is not the direction the government seems inclined to take. The political appetite is for "visible" measures, actions that look tough on paper, such as tightening controls on legal weapon ownership even further. Yet, for the ordinary citizen, these measures are essentially redundant especially when criminals have no intention of following the law to begin with.

As a citizen observing these trends, I am left wondering if this approach reflects genuine public safety concerns or an ideological stance. The focus on civilian disarmament appears motivated, at least in part, by a desire to symbolise control over firearms without addressing the complex realities of modern crime. Criminals exploit regulatory blind spots, and despite layers of legislation, citizens are no less vulnerable. If anything, the current model seems to embolden criminals, who operate with the near certainty that their victims will be unarmed and defenceless.

Ultimately, without a shift in strategy that targets the root causes and networks behind violent crime, the UK's restrictive policies on legal firearm ownership feel largely symbolic. They offer a veneer of control, a means of signalling commitment to safety, but they do little to tackle the intricate web of illicit trade and organised violence that persists unabated.

Reflections on Effectiveness

What becomes apparent through this comparative study is that restrictive laws do not necessarily yield safer societies. The United States, with its Second Amendment freedoms, faces unique challenges in managing gun violence but has also enabled citizens to exercise their right to self-defence. Europe and the UK, with their stringent restrictions, experience lower gun-related homicides but continue to grapple with significant violent crime, often exacerbated by the presence of organised crime and black-market firearms.

This chapter reveals a fundamental issue in gun control policy: an overemphasis on restricting legal ownership while failing to address the underlying causes of crime and the black-market supply of weapons. Whether it's the mass shootings in the United States, gang violence in Europe, or knife attacks in the UK, the evidence suggests that criminals find ways to circumvent the law, leaving law-abiding citizens increasingly defenceless.

The divergent experiences of the USA, Europe, and the UK serve as a reminder that while the control of firearms may address one aspect of public safety, it does not necessarily equate to a reduction in violent crime. The failure of restrictive measures to eliminate criminal access to firearms and other weapons points to a need for a more nuanced approach one that addresses the root causes of violence rather than merely curtailing the rights of citizens to defend themselves.

Chapter 8: The Role of BLACK-MARKET Networks in Evading Gun Control Laws

As governments in the West impose increasingly stringent gun control measures, a hidden marketplace has flourished, supplying firearms to criminals and organised gangs with an efficiency that defies the law. This underground network of black-market operatives is sophisticated, adaptive, and resilient. Despite the best efforts of policymakers and law enforcement, illicit firearms continue to flow into Western societies, feeding criminal enterprises and undermining the very laws designed to protect citizens.

This chapter will examine how black-market networks operate, the strategies traffickers use to evade detection, and the legal loopholes they exploit to sustain an uninterrupted supply of guns. I'll illustrate these points with case studies that highlight the agility of these underground networks in sourcing, smuggling, and distributing firearms. From the smuggling rings operating across the USA-Mexico border to networks trafficking Soviet-era arms from Eastern Europe into Western Europe, these examples reveal a complex and highly profitable ecosystem. I'll also explore how legal grey areas, including the trade in antique firearms and firearm components, provide additional opportunities for criminals to acquire weaponry despite the West's strict regulatory regimes.

The Anatomy of Black-Market Networks: Global Players, Local Impacts

To truly understand the black-market firearm trade, one must first grasp the sheer breadth, sophistication, and resilience of the networks involved. These groups are far from isolated or fragmented; they are well-coordinated and operate with remarkable agility. From sourcing to distribution, these global actors specialise in procuring firearms from often remote and unregulated sources, transporting them across borders, and distributing them to criminal circles with precision. Some of these organisations operate with a level of efficiency akin to military logistics, utilising supply routes that span continents. Over the years, they have perfected the art of smuggling, evolving strategies honed through repeated success in evading national and international authorities alike.

Yet, as I observe the response of Western governments, I am struck by a disconcerting pattern: rather than targeting these sophisticated black-market networks directly, authorities appear far more focused on further restricting access to firearms for ordinary, law-abiding citizens. From my perspective, this approach appears rooted more in ideology or even a troubling lack of political will than in any concerted effort to truly address the flow of weapons to criminals. Across Europe and North America, the focus remains on tightening civilian gun control, despite the overwhelming evidence that these restrictions do little to dent the illegal firearm market.

Consider the trafficking routes stemming from Eastern Europe a region that, since the collapse of the Soviet Union, has become a veritable treasure trove for black-market suppliers. With lax border controls and minimal regulatory oversight, Eastern European nations have become a primary source of surplus firearms, often dating back to the Cold War. These weapons, ranging from handguns to military-grade assault rifles, make their way across multiple borders, moving through well-established routes towards the West, where demand within criminal networks remains high. In cities like Paris, London, and Berlin, law enforcement frequently encounters well-armed gangs equipped with AK-47s, assault rifles, and other high-powered weaponry sourced from this region. These encounters are a stark reminder of the reach and tenacity of these supply chains.

Despite the constant influx of illegal weapons into Western Europe, what I see from governments is a reluctance to tackle the problem at its root. Efforts to increase intelligence-sharing and cross-border law enforcement operations exist in theory, through organisations like Europol, but their impact is limited by bureaucratic inefficiencies and competing national priorities. Meanwhile, security at many European borders remains porous, allowing traffickers to move their goods with relative ease. Initiatives such as "Operation Trigger" have been launched by Interpol and Europol, focusing on firearm trafficking and involving several European countries. Yet these are reactive measures and appear sporadic, with little sustained momentum. In practice, I perceive that the black-market trade has adapted faster than authorities can respond, constantly shifting routes and methods to avoid detection.

Similarly, the situation on the US-Mexico border reveals a critical vulnerability that governments seem ill-prepared to address comprehensively. Here, traffickers exploit the porous nature of the border, which is under immense strain due to issues related to immigration and narcotics. Firearms are smuggled into the United States through routes typically used for drug trafficking, while weapons flow southward into Mexico, where they empower cartels locked in violent struggles for dominance. This bi-directional trade fuels both sides of the border conflict, exacerbating crime and violence in both countries.

Western governments have taken some measures to stem the flow, such as initiatives involving bilateral cooperation between US and Mexican authorities, but these are often hampered by corruption within local agencies and the sheer scale of the problem. Policies targeting legitimate gun dealers have also been implemented in the US, with authorities attempting to clamp down on "straw purchases" where individuals buy guns legally and resell them to criminals. But these measures only scratch the surface of the issue. Despite these limited actions, the government appears more focused on restricting the civilian market a course of action that fails to address the black-market networks driving the violence.

It's frustrating to witness a consistent crackdown on civilian firearm ownership when the real threat comes from these well-organised black-market networks. Many Western leaders, I believe, view stricter gun laws for civilians as a politically palatable solution that appears to "address" gun violence without the complexities of tackling transnational crime networks. Yet, these policies largely serve to disarm ordinary citizens, leaving them more vulnerable, while criminals continue to access sophisticated weaponry with relative ease.

In the case of Eastern Europe, much of the problem stems from under-resourced law enforcement in these source countries, combined with weak legislation governing surplus military weapons. Rather than confronting these core issues, Western countries focus on tightening gun control domestically, leaving criminals free to exploit the gaps in border enforcement and firearm regulation. This reluctance to engage with the black-market networks directly is perhaps a symptom of ideological biases that view civilian gun ownership as inherently dangerous, rather than considering the broader context of illegal firearms that continue to infiltrate Western societies.

Ultimately, the lack of a coordinated, multi-national approach to address the root of black-market firearm trafficking speaks volumes. Despite the existence of frameworks like the European Firearms Directive, there is little evidence to suggest that these policies are effective in curbing the influx of illegal firearms into Western Europe. Enforcement is inconsistent, with nations prioritising domestic gun control over international cooperation on this issue. In the United States, the focus on cracking down on legitimate gun dealers has led to widespread distrust among citizens who feel targeted by a system that appears to ignore the true source of illegal guns: a resilient and well-funded black market.

As a citizen, I am left wondering if the ideological stance against civilian gun ownership blinds our leaders to the actual source of the problem. While law-abiding citizens face ever-increasing restrictions, the criminal underworld continues to thrive, arming itself through networks that governments either cannot or will not disrupt in any meaningful way. In my view, this focus on civilian gun control at the expense of addressing the black market is a misplaced effort that fails to recognise or respond to the realities of firearm trafficking today.

Loopholes and Grey Areas: Exploiting Legal Ambiguities

The scale of loopholes that allow firearms or their components to enter Western markets under the radar is deeply troubling. Despite well-meaning attempts to restrict gun ownership, Western governments seem to overlook the legal grey areas that allow black-market suppliers and criminals to circumvent these laws. One particularly concerning example in the UK is the loophole surrounding antique firearms. Under British law, firearms manufactured before 1900 are classified as antiques and are therefore exempt from the same rigorous controls applied to modern guns. While these exemptions were originally intended to benefit collectors and historians, criminals have found ways to exploit this legal oversight. It is not uncommon to hear of antique firearms being modified, retrofitted with modern components, or otherwise altered to make them operational and lethal once again. This disturbing trend sees weapons, some initially manufactured over a century ago, repurposed into deadly tools in the hands of modern criminals.

There is a marked increase in reports of these antique firearms cropping up in criminal activities, underscoring the need for reforms to address this loophole. Yet, despite the obvious danger posed by this workaround, the government appears slow to respond. Legislation aimed at limiting access to these antique weapons has either stalled or lacks the necessary enforcement measures to be genuinely effective. For instance, while recent reforms require certain types of antique firearms to be registered, there are still many that slip through this regulatory net. As a result, individuals with criminal intent can purchase these "antiques" with little oversight, knowing full well they can be modified into dangerous, functioning firearms.

Another significant weakness in Western gun control laws is the trade in firearm components, which has only expanded in recent years. The UK, among other nations with restrictive laws, tightly controls the sale of complete firearms, making it difficult for individuals to legally obtain a functional gun. However, when it comes to individual components barrels, triggers, magazines, and other essential parts the controls are far less stringent. Criminal networks have become adept at exploiting this regulatory gap. By importing parts separately, often through a network of suppliers in countries with less restrictive firearm laws, they effectively sidestep the prohibitive regulations surrounding assembled guns. Once these parts are smuggled across borders or even acquired within the country, assembling them into a fully operational weapon is simply a matter of expertise and access to tools.

This trend has only accelerated with the rise of online marketplaces and the dark web. On these largely unregulated platforms, individuals can access parts from sellers around the world with little risk of detection. As a result, firearm components can be bought and sold with relative ease, bypassing traditional regulatory scrutiny. Despite the clear evidence that this route is being exploited, governments are often ill-equipped to respond, leaving a glaring gap in the legal framework that black-market operatives continue to exploit.

Consider the ease with which certain parts can enter the country due to gaps in customs and postal checks. The sheer volume of small packages makes it almost impossible for customs officials to inspect each one thoroughly, especially when firearm components are often mislabelled or disguised. A barrel might enter as "machinery," a trigger as "metal components." These deceptive practices allow traffickers to smuggle gun parts into even the most regulated of nations with minimal interference. The government's focus on clamping down on full firearm imports and the legitimate civilian market leaves them blind to the creative methods employed by black-market networks to import what they need to assemble a functional weapon.

Furthermore, recent technological advances in 3D printing have created an additional avenue for criminals to obtain untraceable guns, or "ghost guns," as they are often called. In theory, anyone with access to a 3D printer and a blueprint from the dark web can print essential parts for a firearm, which, when combined with a small number of traditionally manufactured parts, creates a fully functioning gun. While some Western governments have attempted to regulate the distribution of 3D-printed firearm blueprints, enforcement remains a challenge, as these files circulate freely online, often protected by encryption and hosted on offshore servers beyond the reach of domestic law.

And so, what is being done? To my eyes, the actions of Western governments appear fragmented at best. There is a clear reluctance to address these loopholes with the urgency required, perhaps due to a combination of bureaucratic inertia and an ideological focus on limiting civilian gun ownership over tackling the more complex issues posed by black-market operatives. Occasionally, I see isolated initiatives, like the UK's recent efforts to tighten antique firearm classifications and specific customs crackdowns on suspicious imports. However, these measures often feel like stop-gap solutions rather than comprehensive reforms.

The reality remains: these gaps in the law continue to be exploited, and criminals thrive within these grey zones, benefiting from legal loopholes and technological advancements that governments appear unwilling or unable to close effectively. While law-abiding citizens face increasingly restrictive regulations, black-market operatives find ever more inventive ways to skirt the system, empowered by the government's inconsistent and often ideologically skewed response.

If we are serious about reducing gun violence and criminal access to firearms, then Western governments must adopt a far more comprehensive approach. This would require not only tightening regulations around firearm components and 3D printing but also bolstering international cooperation to tackle the transnational nature of these networks. Without such measures, the cycle will continue with increasingly severe restrictions on civilian gun ownership, while criminals exploit the cracks and thrive in the shadows.

Case Studies: The Resilience of Black Market Firearm Networks

The adaptability of black-market firearm trafficking networks is a reality Western governments seem unwilling, or perhaps unable, to address effectively. In the context of today's complex, transnational trafficking systems, the sheer resilience of these operations reveals both the limitations of government interventions and the troubling consequences of this neglect. Let me offer a few cases that illustrate the sophistication of these criminal networks and their uncanny ability to remain several steps ahead of the authorities. These networks operate with calculated precision, exploiting established drug, human trafficking, and now arms trafficking routes that I have documented in previous books on fentanyl and human smuggling.

Take, for instance, the case of an arms trafficking ring based out of Albania, a hotspot for black-market operations with longstanding links to the rest of Europe. In this instance, traffickers sourced firearms from the surplus stockpiles left over from Eastern Europe's Cold War arsenals. Albania and other Balkan states became focal points for weapons smuggling following the fall of the Soviet Union, creating a steady flow of arms towards Western Europe. The network transported weapons through a carefully organised route that ran through several Balkan countries, each with varying degrees of border enforcement and regulatory oversight. By using hidden compartments in vehicles and relying on forged identification, traffickers were able to sidestep customs checks, moving these arms across borders with a level of efficiency and stealth that exposes the weakness of existing EU-wide firearm control measures.

Once these firearms crossed into the heart of Western Europe, they found their way into the hands of organised crime groups and violent gangs. Notably, these groups frequently have ties to other illicit activities, including drug trafficking and human smuggling both trades that further bolster their influence and resources. For example, Albanian criminal networks, long implicated in the trafficking of drugs and humans across the continent, have integrated arms smuggling as a complementary revenue stream, with firearms acting as tools to enforce control within these illicit industries. In a recent instance, law enforcement uncovered an Albanian-run operation that funnelled weapons into France and Germany, where recipients included groups linked to high-stakes drug trafficking. The influx of these firearms into cities such as Paris and Berlin not only fuels street-level violence but also strengthens these gangs' ability to resist and evade law enforcement. The fact that these operations continue largely unabated reveals a persistent failure in EU-wide coordination and enforcement, particularly when it comes to border controls and intelligence sharing.

A similar tale of sophistication and adaptability can be found across the Atlantic. In the United States, black-market networks exploit the southern border with Mexico as an entry point for firearms, mirroring the routes well-trodden by narcotics and human traffickers. This particular network operated in close collaboration with Mexican drug cartels, who not only facilitated the smuggling of firearms into the United States but also used the same well-worn routes to move fentanyl and other synthetic opioids northward. Cartels, whose logistical expertise in drug trafficking is legendary, have applied similar tactics to firearms trafficking, utilising bribery, coercion, and corruption among border officials to ensure smooth passage for their shipments. Corrupt officials willing to look the other way for the right price allow these firearms to infiltrate American cities, adding fuel to the fire of gang violence in areas already plagued by criminal activity.

The situation is exacerbated by the fact that these same networks often have a vested interest in the destabilisation of communities where they operate. By supplying firearms to gangs in urban areas such as Chicago and Los Angeles, these networks not only generate revenue but also create conditions that further enable their drug and human trafficking operations. Law enforcement efforts to intercept these shipments are often hampered by limited resources, political obstacles, and a seeming unwillingness to address the root causes that allow such criminal enterprises to thrive. Border security, while continuously debated, remains inadequate; attempts to improve it are hamstrung by the vastness of the territory and the myriad of established, covert pathways that traffickers continue to exploit.

Despite these well-documented patterns, Western governments seem primarily focused on tightening regulations for law-abiding citizens. In the UK, recent legislation has introduced more stringent requirements for legal gun ownership, placing additional burdens on hobbyists, collectors, and those seeking firearms for legitimate self-defence. The government's efforts to limit access to firearms in the civilian market appear more ideologically driven than rooted in an understanding of black-market realities. Criminals, after all, are not acquiring firearms through licensed shops or hunting clubs they are sourcing them from a global black market that operates with little regard for national laws.

Even the few governmental efforts that do target trafficking routes often feel misdirected or superficial. For instance, increased border checks and anti-trafficking initiatives might disrupt some trafficking networks in the short term, but these efforts rarely address the demand that fuels these networks or the systemic corruption that enables them. Without cooperation among nations, the sharing of intelligence, and an overhaul of customs practices, these measures are unlikely to succeed. Black-market arms networks are skilled at circumventing detection, particularly given the sheer volume of cross-border traffic that makes effective screening a logistical nightmare.

In essence, these criminal networks thrive because they exploit gaps in international cooperation and enforcement, weaknesses in border security, and, perhaps most crucially, an ideological approach by governments that fails to acknowledge the depth of the problem. While law-abiding citizens face increased scrutiny and restrictions, the black-market firearm trade persists, buoyed by resilient and adaptive networks that continue to slip through the cracks. In my view, Western governments must move beyond mere civilian restrictions and adopt a more comprehensive strategy that addresses the true scope of this transnational threat.

The Rise of Technology: 3D Printing and Ghost Guns

The emergence of 3D-printed "ghost guns" has added a new dimension to the black-market firearm trade, challenging the very foundations of current gun control laws. What sets these weapons apart is their lack of serial numbers, making them untraceable and thereby circumventing existing regulatory frameworks entirely. As a citizen observing government responses, I can't help but notice that much of the effort remains targeted at conventional firearms sold through legal channels an approach that completely misses the mark when it comes to addressing the dangers posed by ghost guns. Despite the clear and present threat these firearms represent, Western governments appear ill-prepared, ideologically preoccupied, or perhaps technologically outpaced to tackle this issue head-on.

For instance, 3D printing has made it possible for anyone with the requisite equipment and a set of blueprints (often downloaded from the dark web) to manufacture an entire firearm at home. Unlike traditional firearms, these ghost guns don't require metal parts, which means they can evade traditional detection methods. In some instances, they're constructed almost entirely from polymer, making them undetectable in standard security checks. This poses a stark problem for airports, government buildings, and other locations where conventional metal detectors serve as the primary security measure. Western governments have largely failed to implement the advanced scanning technology required to detect these non-metal firearms at critical entry points, even though this issue has been raised repeatedly by security experts.

The United States serves as a particularly alarming case study. Despite a rise in violent crimes involving ghost guns, efforts to legislate against them have run up against powerful opposition, including from those who argue that such regulation would infringe upon individual privacy rights and freedom of information. The Biden administration, for instance, attempted to mandate that all ghost guns be fitted with serial numbers; however, enforcement of this measure has proven inconsistent and, in many areas, unenforceable. With the digital files used to create these firearms available for anonymous download, any attempt to regulate the production or possession of ghost guns quickly devolves into a game of whack-a-mole, with enforcement agencies perpetually one step behind the criminals they aim to catch.

In Europe, where gun control measures are typically more restrictive, ghost guns pose a slightly different challenge but are no less of a threat. Here, many governments, including the UK, have long relied on stringent background checks, mandatory waiting periods, and firearm licensing as preventive measures. Yet these regulations are rendered useless in the face of 3D printing technology, which allows anyone with the right equipment to sidestep the bureaucracy altogether. The reality is that ghost guns are now surfacing in cases linked to organised crime and gang violence across major European cities. Reports have emerged of gang members in London, Paris, and Berlin using 3D-printed firearms in street violence, further straining police resources already stretched by the broader rise in crime. Despite the growing evidence, European responses have been piecemeal at best, with limited cross-border collaboration to address the spread of ghost gun technology.

To be fair, some efforts are underway. Law enforcement agencies in countries like the UK and Germany are experimenting with advanced scanning technology that can detect certain polymers, and the EU has made gestures towards developing digital controls over blueprints that enable the creation of ghost guns. Yet, such measures feel reactionary and lack a cohesive, forward-thinking approach. The EU's recent moves to restrict the distribution of digital blueprints are difficult to enforce in practice, given the dark web's decentralised nature and the ease with which files can be anonymously shared across international borders. The slow pace of these regulatory efforts is not only outstripped by the rapid evolution of 3D printing technology but is also hampered by bureaucratic delays and ideological disputes over privacy rights and digital freedom.

Some Western governments have begun exploring tighter controls on 3D printing equipment itself, particularly in the United States, where proposals to track sales of high-end printers have been floated. However, such measures raise considerable privacy concerns, and any attempt to limit access to these printers faces resistance from the technology sector, hobbyists, and civil liberties advocates. Even if regulations on 3D printers were successfully implemented, the international nature of the problem would mean that criminals could still procure untraceable firearms from jurisdictions where enforcement is laxer. The global trade in ghost guns like other black-market commodities would likely continue to flourish via cross-border smuggling routes, much as it does today for fentanyl and human trafficking.

The most glaring issue is the ideological hesitancy within Western governments to confront this problem in a unified and forceful manner. While the civilian firearm market endures a litany of new restrictions, it is clear that a significant ideological rift exists over how to handle ghost guns, particularly in the United States, where the debate has become bogged down by partisan divides. Law-abiding gun owners are subject to ever-increasing scrutiny, yet ghost guns, which epitomise the kind of unregulated firearm governments claim to fear most, slip through the cracks. The insistence on regulating civilian ownership rather than adapting to tackle the evolving threat from black-market arms betrays either an ideological bias or a troubling inability to face reality. If Western governments fail to adopt a more comprehensive, adaptive approach to ghost guns, they risk leaving their citizens vulnerable to a growing wave of untraceable weapons that are almost entirely beyond their regulatory reach.

As it stands, the measures that have been implemented are largely symbolic and offer little assurance that governments are addressing the core issues behind ghost guns and their potential proliferation. For as long as policymakers focus on traditional firearms those that already fall under strict regulatory frameworks the spectre of untraceable ghost guns will continue to loom over Western societies, undeterred and largely unchecked.

The Unintended Consequences of Gun Control

The persistence and adaptability of black-market firearm networks reveal an uncomfortable truth: stringent gun control measures, while ostensibly aimed at preventing violence, often fail to achieve their intended outcome. In places like Canada, where gun ownership has been virtually outlawed for private citizens, gun crime among criminals has only increased, underscoring the complex and often counterproductive effects of stringent gun control policies. Instead of reducing violence, these measures appear to create a two-tiered system where law-abiding citizens are disarmed and vulnerable while criminals, thanks to resilient black-market networks, gain increasingly easy access to firearms. This imbalance has led to a vicious cycle in which the failure of gun control laws to curtail crime spurs yet more restrictive regulations, which, in turn, bolster black-market demand.

The situation is as frustrating as it is predictable. For every regulatory hurdle governments impose, traffickers find new, often ingenious ways to circumvent them. For instance, in Canada, the sweeping restrictions have inadvertently driven the firearm trade underground, enriching organised crime networks and fostering an illicit market that operates well beyond government oversight. Criminal gangs are now able to supply firearms with minimal interference, using established smuggling routes from the United States or even sourcing guns through the dark web and private online channels. With the border between Canada and the US stretching over 5,500 miles, traffickers exploit remote areas with minimal law enforcement presence to transport firearms north, often in conjunction with drug smuggling activities. This kind of cross-border trafficking is highly organised, often involving multiple individuals and false documentation to move firearms under the radar. Yet, rather than focus on fortifying these border zones or dedicating resources to disrupt these trafficking routes, the Canadian government has poured resources into sweeping bans and buyback schemes, which have done little to curb the black-market flow.

Western governments, particularly in Europe and North America, often fail to address this issue holistically, neglecting the role of intelligence sharing, border security, and coordinated international enforcement in curtailing the black market. Firearms traffickers, for example, exploit weaknesses in border patrol protocols and logistical blind spots within international postal systems. These weak points allow firearm components to be imported piecemeal, avoiding detection and enabling criminals to assemble weapons once safely within the destination country. In the EU, where firearms trafficking is similarly growing, smugglers frequently use land routes through the Balkans, bringing weapons from Eastern European stockpiles into Western Europe with little interference. These routes have long been used to move other contraband items, such as narcotics, showing how black-market networks capitalise on established criminal logistics channels to move firearms.

Furthermore, technological advances have only exacerbated the problem. In addition to 3D-printed ghost guns, other components, such as solvent traps or so-called "80% lower receivers" (incomplete firearms parts that don't qualify as guns under current laws), are sold legally in some regions and can be converted into functioning weapons with relative ease. Criminals have seized upon these components to create untraceable, home-assembled firearms. Western governments seem unwilling or unable to grapple with this issue, as any legislation targeting these components would demand an agile, cross-border response that currently eludes policymakers. The adaptability of black-market networks makes traditional approaches to gun control seem almost outdated, as though Western policymakers are stuck in the legislative paradigms of the last century.

In addition to these technical and logistical challenges, political ideology often hampers pragmatic solutions. In many Western countries, there exists a deeply ingrained focus on controlling legal firearms owned by civilians, regardless of the evidence that such measures rarely correlate with lower rates of gun crime. This ideological fixation means that the lion's share of enforcement resources is spent policing compliant citizens, while genuine threats continue to operate in the shadows. Take Canada's recent sweeping bans on military-style semi-automatic firearms: although these measures generated considerable media attention and political capital, they left the black-market channels untouched and have done little to stem criminal activity.

If Western governments genuinely aim to protect their citizens from firearm-related violence, they must adopt a more comprehensive, intelligence-led approach that goes beyond simple legislation. Disrupting black-market firearms trafficking requires greater international cooperation, intelligence sharing, and a commitment to addressing systemic weaknesses in border security. Western nations would do well to collaborate with countries that serve as transit or source points for traffickers, engaging in joint enforcement initiatives to dismantle these sophisticated networks. This is especially true for the United States and Canada, where a shared understanding of the cross-border trafficking routes could help prevent firearms from falling into criminal hands.

Ultimately, tackling black-market firearms is not merely a matter of passing new laws; it demands a multi-faceted approach involving legislation, but also intelligence, enforcement, and political will. The question is whether Western governments are willing to transcend ideological preconceptions to craft a solution that acknowledges the adaptive, resilient nature of black-market networks. Until they do, the underground market will continue to thrive, leaving law-abiding citizens at an increased risk while criminals remain armed and emboldened by their success in evading a regulatory system that seems, in many ways, ill-equipped for the modern world.

Chapter 9: The Psychological Impact on Citizens Deprived of Self-Defence

As I dive into this chapter, I aim to confront a profound yet often understated consequence of disarmament policies: the psychological toll on citizens stripped of their right to self-defence. Across many Western countries particularly in Democrat-led U.S. states, the United Kingdom, Canada, New Zealand, Australia, and parts of Europe strict gun control laws have left individuals unable to adequately protect themselves. The rationale for such policies has generally centred on public safety, but there is a deeply ingrained irony here. By disarming law-abiding citizens in the hope of creating safer communities, governments may be fostering a society that feels more vulnerable, more fearful, and increasingly helpless. This unintended consequence felt daily by citizens who find themselves with few options in the face of potential threats threatens the very fabric of public morale and is compounded by the stark reality that criminal access to firearms remains unabated.

Many governments in the West claim that stringent gun control measures are essential to ensure public safety. However, I observe a troubling trend: the overwhelming focus of these policies is on limiting access to firearms for law-abiding citizens, often under the assumption that fewer guns will naturally lead to a reduction in crime. In practice, though, these restrictions appear disproportionately to target those who already comply with the law, while those with criminal intent continue to procure weapons through illegal channels. Measures are passed to make firearm ownership exceedingly difficult, yet they do not seem to curb the proliferation of guns within criminal circles. For instance, in the UK, the police have aggressively targeted legally owned firearms with stringent licencing requirements, mandatory checks, and restrictions on the types of guns that can be owned. While this has effectively reduced civilian ownership, recent years have seen an alarming increase in violent crime, much of which involves weapons trafficked through underground networks or smuggled across porous borders. Criminal gangs and organised crime syndicates thrive on these black-market networks, gaining access to firearms often beyond the scope of police visibility.

In the United States, many states led by Democratic administrations have enacted sweeping reforms aimed at tightening civilian gun laws, implementing policies such as red-flag laws, expanded background checks, and bans on certain types of firearms. Yet, even in cities with the strictest gun regulations, like Chicago and Los Angeles, gun violence persists at alarming levels, fuelled by illegal weapons that flow across state lines or enter through sophisticated trafficking channels. Instead of addressing these networks, policymakers often double down on civilian restrictions, seemingly ignoring the grim reality that criminals are adept at evading these laws. I have noticed that when crime statistics are made public, there is often little acknowledgement of the source of the firearms involved whether they were legally obtained, stolen, or trafficked. This lack of transparency prevents a meaningful public discussion on the actual effectiveness of such policies and leaves many citizens questioning whether these laws are indeed intended to ensure safety or whether they are largely symbolic gestures.

In Australia and New Zealand, sweeping gun bans and buy-back schemes were introduced after mass shootings, with an emphasis on disarming the populace as a path to prevent future tragedies. While these initiatives may have had short-term effects on reducing gun ownership, they have not eradicated gun violence, and the criminal underworld continues to arm itself through illicit means. Australia, for instance, continues to grapple with cases of gang-related shootings, drive-bys, and armed robberies where illegal firearms are used. Yet, public discussions rarely address how these weapons are procured, and instead, the emphasis remains on restricting civilian access.

In Canada, similar policies are at play under the current federal administration, which has been outspoken in its efforts to crack down on civilian gun ownership. The government's approach has involved banning certain types of firearms, implementing magazine restrictions, and launching buy-back programs all under the promise of making Canada safer. However, statistics show a marked rise in gun violence in major cities, with criminals increasingly using smuggled firearms to carry out shootings and gang-related crimes. Rather than targeting the illegal firearms trade, which is facilitated by Canada's extensive border with the United States, policies seem to concentrate on restricting the rights of lawful gun owners, creating a sentiment among citizens that the government is more interested in controlling public ownership than in dismantling the criminal networks profiting from illegal guns.

In the European Union, while strict gun control has long been the norm, countries are still plagued by violence perpetrated with illegal firearms smuggled in from Eastern Europe and the Balkans, where weapons flow from post-conflict regions into Western Europe. Organised crime networks, often highly structured and agile, have established well-worn routes for these firearms, which make their way into cities such as Paris, Brussels, and London. Meanwhile, law-abiding citizens face arduous restrictions that limit their means of protection. In response, authorities tend to implement even tighter gun controls, often with little consideration of the public's growing anxiety over their safety and the failure to address the source of illegal firearms.

For those of us observing these trends, it is difficult to ignore the ideological undertones that often influence these policies. The notion of a "disarmed society" is frequently championed as a moral or progressive ideal, with gun ownership equated with an outdated or dangerous practice incompatible with modernity. This view seems to overlook the reality of criminal behaviour and the sophisticated networks that operate outside legal boundaries. By concentrating efforts on civilian gun control, Western governments, perhaps inadvertently, risk leaving their citizens with a feeling of powerlessness, where trust in the state's ability to protect them dwindles as crime persists unchecked. It raises the question of whether these policies are driven by an ideological commitment to a gun-free society rather than a pragmatic strategy for tackling crime.

The stark reality, then, is that Western governments appear to focus more on controlling the lawful gun market than on targeting the illegal one, often sidestepping the harder task of dismantling black-market networks and criminal syndicates that operate across borders. In effect, citizens are left to shoulder the psychological and practical consequences of policies that disarm them while leaving criminals undeterred. This imbalance breeds a climate of anxiety and disillusionment, where the law-abiding are constrained while criminals operate freely, making it hard to feel genuinely safe in one's community. For many, the trust in the government to provide protection is eroding, and with it, the public morale necessary to maintain a resilient and unified society.

The Role of Self-Defence Rights in Citizen Morale

The right to self-defence has historically been more than just a legal privilege; it is a psychological anchor, offering individuals a degree of control over their safety. Knowing that one can act decisively to defend oneself, one's family and one's property instils a sense of assurance that cannot easily be replicated by any governmental measures or policing efforts. It is not simply a legal entitlement; it is a core component of self-reliance and personal agency. Yet, as Western governments increasingly focus on stringent gun control, this anchor is being eroded, often leaving citizens with an unsettling void, where their fundamental sense of security has been subtly but steadily undermined.

I find it profoundly concerning that the prevailing approach among many Western governments has prioritised a crackdown on civilian gun ownership, while the root of criminal access to weapons is left largely unaddressed. The recent surge in gun violence across major Western cities is a glaring testament to this imbalance. Despite the wealth of evidence pointing to thriving black-market operations, official responses seem almost singularly focused on civilian restrictions, as though disarming lawful citizens will somehow disrupt these illicit networks. In reality, this approach appears misaligned with the problem itself; organised crime syndicates and street gangs do not source their firearms from legitimate markets but from complex smuggling operations and underground trade channels. Yet, it is the law-abiding citizen who feels the brunt of each new wave of restrictions, bearing the loss of a fundamental right that, for centuries, provided reassurance and self-sufficiency.

Western governments, particularly those with stringent left-leaning policy frameworks, seem ideologically committed to the notion that a disarmed populace equates to a safer society. In the United Kingdom, for example, the government has implemented highly restrictive gun ownership laws under the premise that fewer firearms will lead to reduced crime. While these laws have indeed curtailed civilian access, they have done little to diminish the presence of guns within criminal networks. The result is a public left increasingly vulnerable, with limited recourse for personal protection. Official messaging often reinforces the idea that the police are the sole protectors of public safety, yet in many cases, police response times are inadequate to provide timely protection in the face of immediate threats. When citizens are robbed of the means to defend themselves, they are left with little more than the assurance that someone will arrive after the fact, a sentiment that does little to alleviate fears or restore confidence.

In the United States, particularly in states with Democrat-led administrations, the push for gun control has taken on an almost ideological fervour, with a sweeping array of policies aimed at curbing civilian gun ownership. Expanded background checks, limits on magazine capacities, red-flag laws, and outright bans on certain firearm types are all enforced under the auspices of public safety. However, these measures rarely address the flow of illegal weapons that fuel the violence in major cities. The high rates of gun crime in cities with some of the strictest gun laws like Chicago and Los Angeles expose the disconnect between policy intent and practical outcome. The criminal networks that supply these weapons continue to operate with relative impunity, finding ways to exploit legal loopholes or using sophisticated trafficking routes to bring firearms into these urban areas. Yet, the citizenry, especially those in high-crime neighbourhoods, are left with ever-narrowing options for defending themselves, dependent instead on a government that seems unable or unwilling to target the real source of the problem.

In Canada, similar ideological motives have driven the government to implement sweeping firearm restrictions, recently culminating in a ban on certain types of rifles and semi-automatic firearms. In the official narrative, these measures are championed as bold steps towards creating a gun-free society. However, this crackdown on civilian ownership fails to address the mounting issues posed by an active and increasingly well-organised black market. Weapons from the United States and other international sources continue to flow into Canadian cities, supplying gangs and organised crime groups while leaving law-abiding citizens disarmed. The government's solution to this problem has largely been to double down on civilian restrictions, rather than focusing efforts on border security or anti-smuggling initiatives that could more effectively curb the influx of illegal firearms. For many citizens, this policy choice has had a chilling effect on public morale; the implicit message seems to be that the government trusts criminal elements to disarm more than it trusts its populace.

Australia and New Zealand present a similar picture, where government efforts have focused on civilian disarmament, reinforced by buy-back programmes and stringent licensing requirements. These policies emerged from a well-intentioned desire to prevent mass shootings and gun-related violence. However, they have done little to address the continued presence of firearms within the criminal landscape. Gangs in both countries are still able to acquire weapons via smuggling routes, yet citizens are left without viable means of self-protection. In Australia, reports indicate that criminals are often better equipped than the police themselves, creating an environment where the public's trust in state protection is increasingly fragile. Citizens are left wondering if the government's decision to pursue restrictive measures against them, rather than tackling the complex channels that supply criminals, is driven by an ideological reluctance to admit that disarmament has failed to deliver the promised safety.

In Europe, the issue is similarly fraught, with strict gun control policies in countries like France, Germany, and the UK, yet a persistent and rising issue with criminal access to firearms. The majority of these illegal firearms are smuggled in from Eastern Europe and the Balkans, where weapons from past conflicts still circulate through underground channels. Despite this, the response from European governments remains largely focused on limiting civilian access rather than addressing the underlying networks that fuel this influx. In many cases, the police find themselves ill-equipped to combat criminals who possess military-grade weaponry, yet ordinary citizens are expected to place their trust in a system that increasingly appears unable to provide adequate security.

It is this psychological erosion that I find most concerning. By stripping individuals of their right to self-defence and placing all responsibility for safety on the state, Western governments are undermining a vital aspect of personal empowerment. The erosion of self-defence rights sends a powerful, if unintended, message: citizens must surrender their security to an often distant and ideologically driven bureaucracy. As a citizen, I am left questioning whether these policies truly serve the public's best interest, or if they are more about adhering to a vision of society that discounts the realities of human nature and historical precedent. The result is a populace that feels increasingly disillusioned, forced to rely on promises of state protection while seeing little meaningful action to address the criminal elements that persistently threaten public safety. For those of us who value self-sufficiency, this approach is not only inadequate but fundamentally demoralising.

Public Perception of Crime Rates and Fear in Daily Life

Studies across the Western world have shown that fear of crime is often more prevalent than crime itself. Yet this fear is not without basis. While crime rates fluctuate, perception plays a crucial role in shaping how safe people feel, affecting their day-to-day interactions, sense of community, and even mental well-being. A commonly cited report from the British Crime Survey demonstrates that, even as official statistics suggest violent crime has ebbed and flowed, the public's fear often remains high or even escalates despite purported declines. It's ironic that, as officials claim success in reducing crime, the sense of vulnerability among ordinary citizens persists and in some cases, deepens.

In the UK, for example, knife crime has become alarmingly prevalent in major cities, particularly London, and it has intensified public fears over safety in urban areas. Despite repeated government claims that they are "cracking down" on violent crime, the perception on the ground suggests a different reality. Many individuals avoid certain neighbourhoods altogether, particularly at night, and alter their travel routes to avoid public spaces seen as high-risk. With every headline about a new stabbing incident or gang-related altercation, these behaviours become more entrenched. The government has introduced stop-and-search measures as part of its response, yet these efforts appear limited and have sparked significant debate over profiling, casting further doubt on whether these measures address the root of the problem. Rather than instilling confidence, these initiatives often fuel public scepticism, as citizens question if they are truly effective or merely cosmetic.

For those of us living in environments where crime feels on the rise, it's hard to ignore the pervasive sense of unease. In many Western cities, routine activities like walking through a park, waiting for public transport, or even driving through certain areas can feel laden with potential risk. As a result, the average person increasingly invests in self-defence alternatives that do not violate restrictive weapon laws, including expensive home security systems, CCTV, motion sensors, and reinforced locks. It's not uncommon for households to spend thousands of pounds or dollars on these measures, effectively privatising security due to a lack of trust that the public system can fully protect them. The reality, however, is that even with these investments, the psychological toll remains, as the root of the insecurity and the inability to personally intervene in the face of crime remains unaddressed.

In the United States, the situation varies widely by state, but the trend in Democrat-led cities often mirrors that of other Western countries. Many states and cities focus on civilian disarmament, hoping to reduce violence by reducing access to firearms. However, despite stringent gun laws in places like Chicago, New York, and Los Angeles, residents continue to report rising anxiety about personal safety due to persistent street crime, theft, and gang violence. In these cities, the high-profile presence of crime isn't simply a matter of statistics, but of everyday experience incidents that contribute to a narrative of danger that remains unaddressed by the same officials who tout the need for tougher restrictions on self-defence measures. Public policies emphasise that citizens should call the authorities rather than engage, yet response times and limited police resources often leave citizens waiting far too long for any practical intervention.

Governments across the West have indeed sought to reassure the public, frequently citing favourable statistics or presenting heavily qualified interpretations of crime data. Yet, from my perspective, these claims can feel like little more than manipulation, a strategic use of numbers that fails to align with the lived experience of ordinary people. For instance, in the UK, officials may cite a decline in overall crime while failing to acknowledge specific surges in knife-related incidents, burglaries, or violent offences against individuals in certain urban areas. By glossing over these details, they may reduce the visibility of crime on paper but do little to ease the real fears of citizens.

Furthermore, some European countries attempt to counteract public fear by suggesting that better street lighting, increased CCTV coverage, and more community policing will ease the situation. While these measures can offer minor deterrents, they are often insufficient on their own. In many cases, these strategies amount to no more than a veneer of safety a way for officials to say they have done something tangible while leaving deeper issues unresolved. Increased surveillance and lighting can deter minor offences, yet for many citizens, the lack of personal recourse remains troubling. Knowing that CCTV cameras may capture an incident does little to mitigate the immediate threat or to empower individuals with a means to defend themselves.

Australia and New Zealand follow a similar approach, relying heavily on official statistics to support disarmament policies while focusing on increased law enforcement visibility as a primary crime deterrent. Despite this, studies indicate that citizens feel increasingly anxious about rising criminality in certain areas. In response, governments have been hesitant to acknowledge the public's mounting concern, citing instead their successes in limiting access to firearms and reducing specific types of violence. As a result, citizens often feel dismissed or gaslit, experiencing the stark difference between official narratives and their reality. In cities like Melbourne and Auckland, citizens are, in essence, adapting to this perception gap by becoming increasingly self-sufficient in their ways, shifting their lifestyles and personal habits to avoid potential danger zones, and investing in private security measures wherever feasible.

It is deeply concerning that while governments offer sweeping statements about their efforts to protect citizens, the response on the ground remains far less adequate. These policies often look like attempts to reduce incidents on paper rather than genuinely fostering a sense of safety in everyday life. If anything, the disarmament and restrictive measures appear to fuel a self-fulfilling cycle where citizens feel increasingly exposed, unable to engage in even minimal self-defence and ultimately resigned to an environment of distrust. For those of us who see safety as an intrinsic right rather than a privilege conferred by the state, this approach feels not only incomplete but profoundly flawed. It perpetuates a psychological erosion, a slow decline in the confidence and resilience that citizens need to feel secure, further destabilising communities and creating a deeply divided relationship between the public and the state.

Data on Defensive Gun Use and the Feeling of Safety

In regions where defensive gun use is permitted, such as parts of the United States, there is a tangible sense of empowerment among citizens, knowing they have the means to deter crime and protect their families. Studies suggest that civilians use firearms defensively between 500,000 and 3 million times each year, often without a single shot being fired, as the mere presence of a firearm deters would-be attackers. Though these figures are debated, they reveal a significant trend: self-defence serves not only as a mechanism of physical security but also as a form of psychological reassurance, a way of knowing that one is not solely dependent on the state for protection. This contrasts starkly with the reality in the UK, where stringent gun laws prevent law-abiding citizens from carrying firearms for self-defence, leaving the public heavily reliant on police response times which, particularly in rural areas, may be far from timely.

In my youth in the UK, we had a very different approach to crime and punishment. It was an era when justice was not only swift but unambiguous; anyone involved in a crime such as armed robbery faced the full brunt of the law. If a single individual used a weapon in the commission of a crime, every accomplice was charged as if they had wielded that weapon themselves. This collective accountability acted as a powerful deterrent, sending a clear message that participation in violent crime would bring severe consequences. Today, however, the approach feels diluted. We see fewer instances of robust prosecution and a judiciary system that seems to favour rehabilitation over deterrence, even when dealing with serious offences. Sentencing has become softer, and often, it appears as though offenders receive repeated chances rather than facing proportionate penalties for their actions.

Adding to this problem is the wave of mass illegal migration, which has brought untold numbers of individuals into Western nations without comprehensive vetting. Unfortunately, among these migrants are criminals who are not only willing but prepared to use violence to establish control or evade the law. Stories of knife attacks and gang violence involving migrant groups are becoming commonplace in the news, leading to a deeply rooted public anxiety. In the past, border security and immigration processes aimed to filter and assess who entered our countries, but current policies in many Western nations are far laxer. Immigration laws seem to have softened, and in the name of humanitarian efforts, we've inadvertently opened the door to individuals who do not abide by our laws and who bring with them criminal tendencies that endanger the very citizens the state is meant to protect.

Despite these mounting issues, the response from the government and law enforcement is disappointingly inconsistent. There appears to be an unwillingness to address these new criminal elements directly, and rather than focusing efforts on cracking down on those committing violent crimes, we see a disproportionate focus on civilian disarmament. The police, due to policy restrictions or perhaps political influence, are often limited in their ability to act decisively. In cases where migrant-related crime is evident, there seems to be an ideological hesitation a fear of being labelled discriminatory or intolerant that hampers effective law enforcement. As a result, crime committed by recent arrivals is sometimes downplayed or obscured, fostering a narrative that fails to match the reality experienced by everyday citizens.

This reluctance to pursue criminals with the same tenacity we once did only serves to undermine the public's confidence in law enforcement and, ultimately, in the government itself. When people see criminals repeatedly getting away with violent acts, they begin to lose faith in the system designed to protect them. It feels as though the authorities are more intent on controlling and restricting the lawful population than addressing the very real threats posed by an influx of violent offenders. In the UK, recent initiatives have included introducing more police presence in certain urban areas and investing in CCTV to deter crime, yet these measures feel more like surface-level solutions than meaningful reforms. They fail to address the growing fear that many citizens feel, a fear born from a sense of vulnerability and an awareness that, in practice, they are increasingly powerless to protect themselves in the face of criminal threats.

The inability to act on this sentiment is compounded by the inconsistent application of existing laws. Criminals often exploit lenient sentences and an overburdened judicial system, secure in the knowledge that, even if apprehended, their punishment may be far from commensurate with the crime committed. This leniency stands in stark contrast to the treatment of law-abiding citizens who might inadvertently violate minor regulatory laws or self-defence restrictions. In many cases, it feels as if the government and legal system are more focused on ensuring that the public adheres to these ever-tightening restrictions than on dealing with the criminal behaviour that is instilling fear within communities.

The reality is that Western governments, rather than enacting policies that address the root causes of these safety issues, appear to manipulate statistics to reassure the public that crime is under control. By focusing on minor offences, which often inflate crime reduction statistics, they divert attention from the larger, more impactful crimes that truly drive public fear. Meanwhile, violent criminals including those arriving as part of mass illegal migration continue to move within our communities with an alarming degree of impunity. Rather than restoring faith, this approach further undermines the public's trust in government, law enforcement, and the legal system, as citizens witness a seeming unwillingness to address the threats that impact them most directly.

Without significant policy shifts that prioritise prosecuting violent offenders and addressing the realities of mass illegal migration, Western governments risk creating a populace that feels abandoned and betrayed, reliant on a state that can no longer provide the safety and security it promises.

Survey Results on Feelings of Safety

Numerous surveys on public safety reveal an unsettling trend: a growing chasm between what citizens expect from law enforcement and the actual realities of crime prevention. In the UK, recent surveys illustrate this shift starkly, with a significant portion of the population feeling less safe than they did just a decade ago. The headlines are filled with stories of violent incidents on high streets, in public parks, and even in schools, as knife crime continues to rise and gangs become emboldened. It's not merely the frequency of these attacks that is so disturbing, but the sheer brazenness with which they are now carried out. We hear stories of teenagers being stabbed in broad daylight, of elderly individuals attacked without provocation, and of families feeling unsafe simply taking a walk after dark. The effect on the public psyche is profound, fostering a sense that safety can no longer be taken for granted.

Across many European nations, similar sentiments echo. In France, Germany, Sweden, and beyond, we witness a surge in concern over violent crime and gang-related activities, much of which seems tied to social challenges like mass migration, economic disparities, and ineffective integration policies. In these countries, as in the UK, citizens increasingly express fears that go unaddressed by governments who insist that crime statistics show improvement or that violent crime is merely a matter of "isolated incidents." Yet, for the average citizen, such assurances fall flat. The reality they experience, or hear about in their communities, tells a different story. They see towns where petty crime is rampant, where public areas are marred by vandalism and open drug use, and where violence spills into daily life in once unthinkable ways.

The dissonance between public perception and government assurances has thus led to a growing crisis of confidence. Citizens feel that policies around crime prevention do not align with the genuine fears they face. Authorities point to falling crime rates in official reports, yet the methodology often glosses over categories that are most visible and concerning to the public. For instance, a reduction in minor property crime or fraud may indeed reflect progress, but when violent crimes involving knives, firearms, or gang activity appear to be on the rise, such data offers little comfort. People increasingly feel that they are not seeing a comprehensive response to crime, especially as governments often focus on initiatives that, to citizens, seem out of touch with pressing threats on the ground.

One aspect of this crisis of confidence lies in the perception of government priorities. In the UK, the emphasis on reporting minor infractions, such as hate speech violations online or regulatory breaches, feels starkly disproportionate to the threats posed by violent criminals. Citizens feel frustrated watching limited police resources diverted to pursue social media posts or low-level regulatory issues while violent crime in their neighbourhoods appears unchecked. In some cases, it feels as though law enforcement is more concerned with policing speech or enforcing trivial regulations than with tackling the immediate dangers presented by gangs or knife crime. This imbalance undermines public trust; rather than feeling protected, citizens feel as though their concerns are deprioritised, replaced by ideological or politically expedient agendas that bear little relevance to their daily lives.

Moreover, there is an increasing perception that political correctness has infiltrated the realm of law enforcement, deterring authorities from addressing certain types of crime head-on. For instance, discussions surrounding the intersection of violent crime and mass migration are often downplayed or ignored entirely in public discourse, creating a sense that the government is unwilling to confront difficult truths. Citizens feel that these realities are softened to avoid difficult conversations, even as crime in certain areas rises. This unwillingness to confront the sources of public anxiety, compounded by a reluctance to address issues of integration, fuels the impression that authorities are neither listening to nor acting on the concerns of those they are meant to serve.

In this atmosphere of diminished trust, more and more people are taking their safety into their own hands. While still limited in the UK due to strict weapon laws, we increasingly see individuals installing advanced security systems, reinforcing doors and windows, and adjusting their daily routines to avoid areas perceived as unsafe. This phenomenon is, in itself, a testament to the lack of confidence in the state's ability to protect its citizens. People should not have to avoid certain neighbourhoods, refrain from public transport after dark, or feel compelled to invest in extensive home security just to feel marginally safer. Yet, that is the reality many now face, and it is a far cry from the assurances of safety once taken as a given.

The perception of an "out of touch" government extends to policymaking. For example, discussions around crime often seem to focus on prevention through community initiatives and outreach programmes, which, while valuable, do not address the immediate and visible threat posed by entrenched criminal networks. Citizens frequently ask why harsher sentences, more stringent law enforcement, or visible police presence aren't prioritised. In the eyes of many, these are tangible measures that directly address the concerns around crime, yet such responses are often cast aside in favour of policies that, while idealistic, do not offer immediate security. In short, while governments emphasise rehabilitation and community building, the public is left feeling as though the basic promise of safety has been sacrificed.

Ultimately, this crisis of confidence is reshaping the social fabric. When citizens no longer feel assured of their safety, a kind of societal fragmentation takes hold. Neighbourhoods become less open, and people become wary of their surroundings and each other. Public morale erodes as people feel abandoned by the very institutions meant to safeguard their welfare. This shift is subtle yet profound, as it impacts how people view their roles as citizens, eroding the sense of community that is essential for societal cohesion. If governments are to regain the trust of the public, they must address this divide head-on, acknowledging not only the statistical measures of crime but the lived experiences of fear and vulnerability that now characterise life for so many citizens across the West.

The Psychological Toll of Vulnerability and Its Impact on Social Behaviour

Being unable to protect oneself has far-reaching consequences. It transforms daily life, often subtly, into a series of cautious choices. Those who feel vulnerable may avoid public transport, alter their walking routes, or hesitate to socialise in certain areas. As these behaviours become widespread, cities can lose their vibrancy and sense of community. Furthermore, distrust builds towards governmental authorities, seen as incapable of balancing the right to safety with an individual's right to defend oneself.

Over time, individuals who feel perpetually vulnerable may develop a form of societal detachment, where they disengage from community involvement and avoid activities that once brought them joy. The absence of self-defence rights affects not only their sense of safety but also their participation in society. This withdrawal weakens the social bonds that are crucial for a cohesive and resilient community.

The psychological impact of disarmament on citizens is a multifaceted issue with profound consequences. While the stated intention behind stringent gun laws is to reduce violence, one cannot help but question whether there is another agenda at play: a gradual erosion of individual empowerment in favour of state control. These laws, though ostensibly about safety, have left citizens feeling powerless in the face of very real threats. There is an unsettling irony in a government that professes to protect its people while, at the same time, stripping away their means to protect themselves. Whether intended or unintended, the effect is palpable a pervasive sense of helplessness, as individuals find themselves exposed to criminal elements that they have no real way of countering. For many, it feels less like protection and more like a restriction, a leash tethering citizens to the state's mercy and assuming that police presence can act as a proxy for personal security.

This situation is particularly disquieting in rural areas or parts of cities where police response times are far from immediate. In these settings, the disarmament of law-abiding citizens feels almost punitive, as if they are expected to simply wait often tens of minutes or even hours for help to arrive in the event of an emergency. In the meantime, they are left defenceless, hoping that whoever has broken into their home, assaulted them in the street, or threatened their loved ones will not escalate their attack. In the past, the ability to wield even a small measure of force, whether through firearms or non-lethal means, served as a psychological anchor. It provided citizens with a sense of control over their safety, allowing them to sleep a little sounder at night, knowing they were not solely dependent on the unpredictable and often delayed arrival of police assistance.

Moreover, when I examine this shift toward disarmament, I notice that it tends to ignore or even sidestep the realities of criminal behaviour. Criminals, by their very nature, disregard the law, and stringent regulations mean little to those already inclined to violence. Instead, these laws appear to apply only to the very people most willing to abide by them law-abiding citizens. This creates a chilling imbalance, wherein the law-abiding are left vulnerable, while criminals, many of whom have easy access to black-market firearms or other weapons, continue to operate with impunity. It seems an extraordinary oversight, one that leaves everyday people exposed while authorities insist that disarmament is for the public good.

The effects of these policies reach deeper than mere inconvenience; they foster a culture of dependence on the state, where citizens are expected to place their trust in an institution that they may see failing to protect them adequately. I cannot help but wonder whether this dependency is, at least in part, the intended outcome. As citizens become reliant on a "protective" state, they gradually lose the sense of self-reliance that has historically been a hallmark of personal freedom. Governments that genuinely value freedom should, in theory, empower individuals to protect themselves, not enforce reliance on government intervention at every turn. Yet, what we see is an environment where self-defence is not only discouraged but often penalised, sending the message that only the state has the authority to determine who may or may not feel secure.

This sense of reliance is even more pronounced when we consider the broader ideological trends behind these policies. In certain circles, the very notion of self-defence is viewed as archaic, a relic of a more "primitive" society that has no place in modern times. This view, however, disregards the genuine fears and practical concerns of those who must live in the reality of modern crime, where violent offenders roam freely, often emboldened by the knowledge that their potential victims are unlikely to be armed. By dismissing the validity of self-defence, policymakers inadvertently endorse a model of society where passivity is encouraged, and individual responsibility is replaced by total reliance on the state. It's a vision of public safety that seems increasingly disconnected from the daily lives and genuine concerns of ordinary citizens.

This ideological approach, which often frames self-defence as a threat to civil society rather than a safeguard within it, ultimately weakens the very fabric of public morale. It creates a division between those who make the laws and those who must live with the consequences of them. Citizens, especially those in areas where crime rates have surged, understandably question the logic of policies that claim to keep them safe while rendering them defenceless. When the state's solution to crime is to render its populace unable to act in their defence, one wonders whether public safety is truly the aim, or if it is, in fact, about control.

This dynamic is not lost on the populace. People notice that while they are told to disarm, criminals continue to have access to weapons and little is done to clamp down on the illegal arms trade that fuels violent crime. The message this sends is unmistakable: the law-abiding are to be held back, restricted, and made to feel powerless, while those who would do them harm face fewer and fewer deterrents. It is a deeply troubling scenario, one that I believe warrants serious reflection. Are we genuinely safer, or have we merely traded the illusion of safety for a reality of vulnerability, all while the state expands its grip on the notion of "protection" it offers to an increasingly disillusioned public? This is the question that arises when the balance of power shifts so decisively away from the citizen and into the hands of the state.

Chapter 10: Policy Critiques: Analysing the Failures of Current Gun Control Approaches

The landscape of gun control in the West has become a battleground of ideas, ideologies, and, often, deeply flawed policies. As I explore the failures of current approaches, it is crucial to step back from political posturing and examine what these policies have, and have not, achieved. In this chapter, I analyse the weaknesses embedded within the current legislative frameworks, drawing on studies, expert opinions, and documented outcomes to uncover the gaps in implementation, enforcement, and adaptation to contemporary threats. A core issue lies in how politicians and policymakers champion restrictive laws while failing to account for criminal realities, resulting in a society divided between lawful citizens whose rights are curtailed and a criminal underworld that has only grown more daring.

Failures in Implementation and Enforcement

One of the most glaring weaknesses in current gun control policies is the chasm between legislation and its enforcement. Gun control laws, however well-intentioned, are ultimately only as effective as their execution on the ground. Yet, many Western countries lack the resources, manpower, and technological infrastructure to enforce these laws effectively, allowing criminals to acquire firearms with alarming ease while law-abiding citizens face a maze of restrictions. This systemic failure – the disconnect between what is legislated and what is practicable – not only undermines public safety but also erodes trust in government institutions.

To illustrate, one of the most common critiques from both law enforcement bodies and criminologists is the inadequacy of resources allocated for enforcement. For example, stringent background checks are often cited as a cornerstone of gun control, but in reality, they are only as comprehensive as the databases that support them. In many countries, these systems are fragmented, with different police jurisdictions maintaining separate databases that are rarely fully synchronised or updated in real-time. A 2019 report by the United Nations Office on Drugs and Crime highlighted this challenge, showing that Western nations are increasingly unable to effectively implement background checks due to gaps in data sharing and slow information processing across regions. The result is a porous system in which background checks that could prevent known criminals from purchasing firearms often fail to do so due to clerical delays or missing data.

The technology used in these checks is itself another obstacle. Many enforcement agencies operate on outdated software systems that cannot handle modern data loads or complex background scenarios. Unlike private-sector databases, which are frequently updated, government databases are often bogged down by bureaucracy and lack the interoperability to function across national and local boundaries. In the United Kingdom, for instance, numerous police forces have reported using antiquated computer systems, some dating back over a decade, which cannot effectively communicate with newer platforms employed by other agencies. This lack of technological integration makes it incredibly difficult for background checks to be thorough or efficient, and criminals can, at times, exploit these loopholes.

The problem of enforcement is compounded by a shortage of manpower, particularly in areas where firearm crime is most prevalent. In cities such as London, Manchester, and Birmingham, police forces are often stretched thin, with officers tasked to cover multiple roles due to funding cuts and recruitment challenges. The consequences are particularly stark in terms of monitoring and interdiction of illegal firearm trafficking. Police simply do not have enough personnel to follow up on every lead regarding illegal arms smuggling or possession, nor do they have sufficient resources to deploy dedicated teams to track firearm transactions on the black market.

For instance, a report from the London Metropolitan Police in 2021 indicated that over half of the gun-related crimes in the capital involved illegal weapons brought in through underground networks, typically originating in Eastern Europe. The report also noted that police units dedicated to intercepting illegal firearms are significantly under-resourced, leading to a "reactionary" approach rather than a proactive one. Officers primarily respond to incidents after they occur, rather than actively disrupting trafficking routes or pursuing smuggling networks.

Indeed, Western countries' enforcement bodies face complex challenges in managing the inflow of illegal firearms, which significantly contributes to the arsenal available to criminal elements. Even in jurisdictions with some of the strictest firearm regulations, such as the United Kingdom, black-market arms are readily available. In urban centres, firearms are often more accessible to those with criminal intentions than to law-abiding citizens, a grim irony in light of the laws intended to prevent precisely this imbalance.

The same can be observed in other Western countries. In France, for instance, the firearm black market is particularly active, with firearms from the Balkans and North Africa smuggled into the country through well-established routes. French authorities are fully aware of these routes and trafficking methods; however, they lack the necessary enforcement personnel and cross-border cooperation to dismantle these networks effectively. As a result, illegal firearms flood the streets of Paris, Marseille, and Lyon, empowering organised crime networks and putting law-abiding citizens at greater risk.

Furthermore, this accessibility of firearms to criminal groups raises serious questions about the efficacy of strict gun control laws when they only seem to restrict the freedoms of those who would comply with them. Criminals operate with near impunity, exploiting loopholes and deficiencies in enforcement, often well aware of the limitations police face. In contrast, law-abiding citizens are often unable to obtain the means to protect themselves and their families due to restrictive policies that limit private firearm ownership or impose burdensome bureaucratic procedures on those who wish to acquire a firearm legally.

This situation has effectively created two classes within society: the law-abiding citizens who must navigate an ever-tightening noose of restrictions to comply with gun laws, and the emboldened criminal underworld, which has ample access to firearms through illegal means. For example, recent studies in Canada, a country with highly restrictive firearm laws, show a significant rise in firearm-related violence despite stringent regulations. Police reports indicate that nearly 80% of gun-related crimes involve illegal firearms, typically smuggled in from the United States. Despite Canada's strict legislation, the black market has flourished, underscoring the point that laws restricting firearm ownership among lawful citizens do little to prevent criminal access to guns.

In the United States, the challenges are further complicated by the country's unique federal structure, where states have significant autonomy over their gun laws. While some states have enacted stringent gun control measures, neighbouring states may have far more permissive regulations. Criminals can exploit these discrepancies, moving firearms across state lines with relative ease. Federal efforts to establish universal background checks or inter-state tracking mechanisms often encounter opposition or legal hurdles, further fragmenting the enforcement landscape. This has led to scenarios where cities with strict gun laws, such as Chicago, face high rates of gun violence due in part to the easy availability of firearms in nearby states with more lenient regulations.

Such deficiencies in enforcement are compounded by the fact that policies are often reactionary rather than proactive, implemented in response to public outcry following high-profile incidents of gun violence rather than through measured analysis of enforcement gaps. Following mass shootings or spikes in gun-related crime, governments frequently push for increased restrictions on firearm ownership without necessarily bolstering the tools, personnel, and coordination required for enforcement. This reactionary approach results in hasty legislation that does not fully account for the enforcement challenges and frequently overlooks existing vulnerabilities in gun control measures.

Ultimately, this lack of effective enforcement turns legislative intention into little more than an empty promise, creating a regulatory framework that cannot hold up under the realities of modern criminal activity. The intention behind gun control laws is to create safer societies, but without sufficient resources to enforce these laws, they remain largely symbolic – incapable of stopping the inflow of illegal arms or providing meaningful deterrence against criminal possession of firearms.

This critique of enforcement highlights the need for policy overhauls that take into account the practicalities of policing and the complexities of gun trafficking in a globalised world. There is an urgent need for better-coordinated efforts across national and international borders, including stronger intelligence-sharing networks and more robust technological tools for tracking illegal firearm movements. A focus on bolstering the practical capabilities of law enforcement, from better training to technological upgrades, is essential if the intentions of gun control legislation are to be realised in practice.

Inflexibility and Inadequate Adaptation to Modern Threats

Gun control policies in the West, at least in their current forms, seem woefully inadequate to address the shifting landscape of threats that have emerged in recent years. Traditional policies, largely crafted in an era when firearms trafficking followed relatively predictable paths, now struggle to contain the modern complexities of organised crime, digital black markets, and the advent of untraceable weapons. In many ways, these policies feel like relics of a past that no longer aligns with today's far more sophisticated criminal networks, which operate on a global scale, bolstered by rapid advances in technology and increasingly well-organised trafficking routes.

One of the most glaring examples of these inadequacies lies in the rise of untraceable "ghost guns" and 3D-printed firearms, which are fundamentally reshaping the nature of gun control challenges. Traditional gun laws often hinge on the control of licensed manufacturers, regulated retail spaces, and firearms with serial numbers. Yet ghost guns, which can be assembled from kits sold online or manufactured entirely from parts created with 3D printers, circumvent these controls entirely. Without serial numbers or registration, they are effectively invisible to the tracking systems that are central to Western gun control strategies. In the United States, these unregulated weapons have already shown their capacity to enter criminal networks with little hindrance, and although some attempts at regulation have been introduced, enforcement remains challenging due to the decentralised and discreet nature of their production.

The emergence of 3D-printed firearms adds another layer of complexity. In theory, anyone with access to a 3D printer and the right digital files can manufacture a firearm within the privacy of their own home, entirely bypassing legal channels. Unlike traditional firearms, which require smuggling and trafficking networks to reach criminal hands, 3D-printed guns can be produced locally, creating an unprecedented challenge for law enforcement. At present, there are few meaningful barriers to downloading schematics for these weapons, many of which circulate freely on the dark web. The files themselves, much like any digital information, can be transferred globally in an instant, moving beyond the reach of national legislation and jurisdictional boundaries. Yet Western gun control policies remain largely silent on this issue, with lawmakers lagging in crafting regulations that address this novel threat.

The evolution of organised crime networks has only compounded the problem. Once operating in defined territories and engaging in predictable patterns of trafficking, organised criminal groups have become increasingly networked across international borders. Many of these networks now have the resources to bypass national regulations entirely, relying on sophisticated supply chains that crisscross continents. Arms trafficking, in particular, has grown into a global business, often conducted alongside human trafficking and drug smuggling operations. Groups in Eastern Europe, the Balkans, and South America have become some of the most prolific suppliers of illegal firearms, utilising established smuggling routes to bring weapons into Western Europe and North America. These weapons find their way into urban centres, often beyond the reach of local law enforcement, who lack the resources and jurisdictional authority to intercept international shipments effectively.

Further exacerbating this issue is the rise of online marketplaces and dark web transactions, which now serve as virtual arms bazaars beyond the reach of conventional enforcement. Platforms such as Silk Road and its successors have demonstrated the potential for digital markets to provide a vast, anonymous platform for arms trafficking. Transactions on the dark web are facilitated by cryptocurrencies, making payments nearly impossible to trace. Weapons can be purchased with the click of a button, often shipped in parts or disguised within legal items to evade detection at customs. Unlike traditional firearm purchases, which involve physical inspection, paperwork, and background checks, dark web transactions are decentralised, anonymous, and borderless – effectively rendering the traditional methods of gun control obsolete. Western gun control policies, built around brick-and-mortar models of firearm acquisition and trafficking, have not kept pace with these technological advancements. The result is a patchwork approach that fails to address the underlying issue: that firearms are increasingly obtainable without setting foot in a regulated gun shop.

This is where the lack of technological adaptation in the West's gun control infrastructure becomes most evident. Even though much of today's firearm trafficking occurs in virtual spaces, Western law enforcement agencies often lack the cyber capabilities required to combat this form of trafficking effectively. While some countries have invested in cybersecurity and digital policing units, these efforts are uneven across jurisdictions and often limited by budget constraints. In the UK, for example, police forces have repeatedly called for increased funding to combat cybercrime, but the resources allocated to these units are typically stretched thin. The need for skilled personnel, specialised technology, and ongoing training in this rapidly evolving field remains largely unmet, leaving significant gaps in the West's ability to monitor and regulate online firearms trafficking.

Moreover, the failure to update policies to address these developments highlights a broader disconnect between existing laws and the realities of the 21st century, where crime has increasingly become a digital challenge as much as it is a physical one. In an age where criminal networks are adept at using encrypted messaging, blockchain technology, and anonymous online platforms, Western gun control laws, based on a much simpler world, seem hopelessly outdated. To be effective, modern gun control must evolve to target not only physical trafficking routes but also the virtual landscapes where arms trafficking now thrives.

The consequences of these policy failures are stark. Criminals can obtain firearms with relative ease, while law-abiding citizens are subject to increasing restrictions and bureaucratic hurdles in accessing legal means of self-defence. This imbalance not only emboldens criminal groups but also undermines public trust in the efficacy of gun control measures. In some urban centres, particularly in North America, firearms are more accessible to those with criminal intent than to those seeking legal protection. A regulatory environment that fails to consider the rapid evolution of trafficking methods and the digital nature of modern crime effectively handicaps itself, rendering legislative intentions ineffective.

What is needed, then, is a wholesale reconsideration of gun control policies that account for the complex, interconnected nature of modern crime. This could include a focus on cross-border cooperation, creating international databases for tracking firearms and their components, and enhancing cyber capabilities for law enforcement. Rather than simply tightening regulations on legal firearm ownership, Western countries must invest in intelligence-sharing networks, cybercrime units, and technologies that allow real-time tracking of digital transactions. As gun violence and trafficking continue to adapt to the digital age, so too must the policies designed to curb them. Only then can Western nations hope to bridge the gap between policy and practice, building a system that is both comprehensive and adaptable to the ever-shifting landscape of modern threats.

Political Motivations and a Disconnect from Criminal Realities

A core issue with the current approach to gun control in Western nations is that these policies are often rooted more in political posturing than in a substantive understanding of criminal behaviour or the everyday realities facing citizens. In many cases, the primary motivation behind restrictive gun legislation seems to be the appearance of taking decisive action, rather than confronting the complex network of issues that underpins gun violence. Politicians, eager to showcase progress in reducing crime, often promote restrictions that may sound effective in speeches or look convincing in legislative documents, yet fail to consider the practical challenges of enforcement or the real-life consequences for law-abiding citizens. The result is a collection of policies that hinder responsible citizens' ability to protect themselves while doing alarmingly little to disrupt the activities of the criminal underworld.

Take, for example, the gun control policies in major cities like London, which has some of the most stringent gun laws in the world. Despite these laws, London's gun crime rates remain persistently high, with violent offences involving firearms surging in recent years. Metropolitan Police Commander Paul Brogden has revealed that approximately one firearm is seized from London's streets every day, with the majority of incidents linked to gang activity or organised crime networks. The drive for control over territory, the settling of debts, and the flow of drugs and money all fuel an entrenched cycle of violence. Recent data from the Office for National Statistics (ONS) revealed a troubling rise in overall gun crime in London, with offences increasing from 1,009 in the year ending December 2022 to 1,208 in the same period last year. For all the government's focus on restrictions, these figures make it clear that stringent gun control policies have failed to address the realities of organised crime, which continues to operate undeterred.

This persistent cycle of violence, despite ever-tightening restrictions, lays bare a central problem: policymakers often ignore the fact that criminals, by definition, are unlikely to be deterred by regulations that only affect lawful citizens. Criminals acquire firearms through illegal channels, including black markets and international trafficking networks that are beyond the reach of conventional enforcement. The bureaucratic processes of obtaining a firearm licence, meeting legal requirements, and registering one's weapon mean nothing to a gang member or organised criminal. They don't need to navigate these regulatory mazes because their means of acquisition exist outside the system. Yet, these restrictions bear heavily on law-abiding citizens, whose access to self-defence options becomes increasingly curtailed.

In cities across Europe and North America, a similar trend emerges, where stringent gun laws appear to exacerbate citizens' frustration and sense of vulnerability. Many of these cities are marred by rising crime rates, yet local populations feel as though their means of protection are becoming progressively limited. This disconnection between policy intent and real-world impact is a source of deep disillusionment for communities, who increasingly question whether these restrictions are serving their best interests. In urban centres like Chicago or Paris, for instance, citizens witness rising violence even as new gun laws are introduced. There is a growing perception that politicians are more concerned with signalling a "tough on crime" stance than in genuinely addressing the criminal behaviours that give rise to gun violence in the first place.

One critical misstep in these policies is the failure to recognise and address the complex socioeconomic conditions that contribute to crime. Poverty, lack of education, and limited economic opportunity create fertile ground for criminal networks, particularly in inner-city areas where young people may see gang affiliation as a viable path to survival or status. By concentrating solely on the tool of the firearm rather than on the motivations that lead individuals into criminal activity, these laws fail to disrupt the cycle of violence that drives gun crime. The assumption that restrictive firearm policies will reduce gun violence is misguided if the policies do not also address the socioeconomic factors that push individuals towards crime in the first place. Indeed, some of the most crime-ridden neighbourhoods are also those most marginalised by policy decisions that ignore the need for educational investment, employment opportunities, and community development.

Furthermore, gun control policies frequently suffer from a disconnect with local law enforcement. Police forces, who are on the front lines of tackling crime, often find themselves at odds with restrictive gun laws that are impractical to enforce effectively. Officers understand the realities of gun crime in a way that legislators who rarely set foot in the affected communities often do not. Many law enforcement officials argue that resources would be better spent on targeted anti-gang operations, community outreach, and early intervention programmes, rather than on enforcing regulations that predominantly impact those already inclined to comply with the law. In some cases, stringent gun laws may even strain police-community relations, as citizens who feel unfairly restricted begin to view law enforcement as complicit in their disempowerment.

Another striking example of the limitations of these policies is the response or lack thereof to the burgeoning market for untraceable weapons. Criminal organisations have shown remarkable adaptability, exploiting new avenues to obtain weapons without falling afoul of conventional gun laws. The rise of ghost guns and 3D-printed firearms illustrates this adaptability clearly. Politicians, eager to create visible restrictions on legal gun ownership, rarely address the ease with which these untraceable weapons can be procured and assembled. The legislative focus on restricting licensed firearm sales does nothing to address the black-market alternatives available to criminal groups. This short-sighted approach neglects the fact that as long as there is a demand for firearms, those determined to obtain them will find a way to do so, regardless of how restrictive the laws become.

In essence, these gun control policies appear rooted in a misguided assumption that the imposition of additional restrictions will curtail the activities of those who are most intent on causing harm. Instead, they have largely resulted in symbolic victories and legal measures that look impressive on paper but achieve little in practice. Such laws may serve to bolster the political profile of those who pass them, but they leave citizens feeling more vulnerable and frustrated. Meanwhile, the real problems entrenched in organised crime, socioeconomic disadvantage, and the inadequacy of resources for local enforcement are left unaddressed.

What Western gun control needs is not more symbolic legislation but a pragmatic shift in focus towards tackling the conditions that allow gun violence to proliferate. This could include investment in community-based interventions, a stronger focus on combatting the trafficking networks that supply illegal weapons, and a commitment to addressing the socioeconomic conditions that contribute to crime. By continually focusing on restrictive measures that affect only lawful citizens, policymakers are missing the opportunity to pursue a more nuanced, comprehensive approach. Until this shift is made, gun control policies will continue to be perceived not as solutions, but as politically motivated gestures gestures that come at a high cost to the safety and trust of the public.

Legislative Shortcomings: An Unintended Boost to the Criminal Underworld

Restrictive gun policies, despite their well-intentioned aim to curb gun violence, have instead fostered a perverse environment in which criminal organisations thrive on the monopoly of arms trafficking. Just as we saw with alcohol prohibition in the United States, the outlawing or restriction of a heavily sought-after commodity inevitably spawns a parallel economy, dominated by those willing to circumvent the law. The black market in firearms has thus become not only an unintended byproduct but a direct beneficiary of strict gun regulations. In a society where legal avenues for acquiring a firearm are limited to the point of inaccessibility for ordinary citizens, criminal networks have emerged as the primary suppliers for anyone willing to pay the price often individuals with malicious intent. In this way, restrictive policies do not eradicate guns; they simply transfer control of firearms to unregulated hands.

In today's world, where globalised supply chains and digital communication have streamlined nearly every aspect of trade, criminal networks exploit gun restrictions to an unprecedented degree. These networks now operate sophisticated, transnational systems capable of sourcing, trafficking, and distributing firearms with relative ease. With borders increasingly difficult to secure and enforcement stretched thin, black-market arms dealers can source weapons from countries with less stringent controls, smuggle them into more restrictive jurisdictions, and sell them at inflated prices to those desperate enough to pay. Far from restricting firearm access, these policies have given organised crime syndicates a new, highly profitable venture. The economic incentives for traffickers are immense: each additional legal restriction on firearm sales inflates the price and demand for black-market arms, fortifying the power and reach of these networks.

A troubling aspect of this dynamic is that criminal organisations have grown adept at manipulating regulatory differences between jurisdictions. European countries, for instance, often have highly varied gun laws. Traffickers exploit these disparities by sourcing weapons from regions with looser regulations and then transporting them across borders into heavily restricted areas. This "patchwork" effect not only highlights the inability of restrictive laws to contain firearms within borders but also points to the fundamental flaw in a model that aims to isolate countries from the international firearms trade. Without cohesive, transnational anti-trafficking cooperation, localised restrictions serve little more than to make black-market arms more profitable.

The digital age has only expanded these illegal supply channels. Online marketplaces, especially on the dark web, have transformed the way criminals access firearms, creating anonymous platforms where weapons are traded, sourced, and shipped globally with few obstacles. Unlike legal transactions, which come with extensive background checks, waiting periods, and registration requirements, purchases on the dark web are swift and shielded from scrutiny. This shift towards digital transactions further undermines the aims of restrictive gun policies, as the very measures intended to "control" firearms push individuals toward these virtual black markets, which operate far beyond the reach of conventional law enforcement.

In these markets, the influx of so-called "ghost guns" firearms that can be assembled at home from parts without serial numbers or identifying marks has added yet another layer of complexity. The criminal underworld capitalises on these weapons, which can evade detection by traditional tracking methods. Parts for these guns are often legal to purchase and can be imported under innocuous descriptions, making it exceedingly difficult for authorities to intercept their entry into restricted areas. Consequently, these untraceable weapons often end up in the hands of criminals, further weakening any notion of control over firearm distribution.

This bleak reality creates a paradox for law-abiding citizens. Those who would seek firearms for legitimate self-defence face rigorous background checks, extended waiting periods, and, in some cases, outright denials. Conversely, those with criminal intent have no such barriers, as they can procure weapons swiftly from the criminal marketplace, equipped with the resources, networks, and know-how to evade scrutiny. For individuals attempting to protect themselves and their families, the hurdles posed by restrictive gun laws create a frustrating and potentially dangerous imbalance. Law-abiding citizens, left unarmed or facing endless red tape, find themselves relying on under-resourced police forces for protection, often in communities already stretched by high rates of crime.

The knock-on effects of these policies extend further into society. By funnelling resources into the enforcement of stringent gun laws, policymakers inadvertently divert attention and funding from the broader crime-fighting initiatives that could disrupt the criminal networks responsible for trafficking firearms. Instead of investing in intelligence, border security, and community-oriented policing, governments frequently prioritise policies that focus on restricting lawful firearm ownership. This imbalance weakens law enforcement's ability to effectively target the root of gun violence: organised crime. Resources that might otherwise be used to track, infiltrate, and dismantle these networks are instead allocated towards ensuring compliance among the general populace citizens who are not contributing to the problem of gun violence.

In effect, restrictive gun policies have turned gun control into a battle of optics rather than outcomes. Politicians herald these laws as steps toward public safety, yet the reality on the ground is that these restrictions often leave citizens feeling less secure and more disillusioned. Criminal organisations, meanwhile, are emboldened by a system that inadvertently bolsters their power, gives them greater control over the market, and reduces their competition to law-abiding individuals. In this environment, the intentions of restrictive policies become almost irrelevant, as the unintended consequences namely, the empowerment of the criminal underworld become increasingly difficult to ignore.

If there is any path to a truly safer society, it lies not in making firearms harder for law-abiding citizens to access, but in directly targeting the supply chains and networks that funnel illegal weapons into our communities. We must prioritise enforcement measures that address the core of the problem, focusing on dismantling the criminal organisations and illicit supply routes that fuel gun violence. Rather than restricting access for responsible citizens, policymakers should consider a balanced approach that strengthens security at borders, invests in technology to trace and intercept trafficking, and enhances international cooperation. Only by addressing these underlying factors can we hope to counter the monopoly that criminal networks currently enjoy in the firearms trade a monopoly created, ironically, by the very policies meant to protect us.

The Fragmentation of Society and the Erosion of Trust in Governance

Gun control policies, when poorly aligned with the realities of public safety, serve not only to infringe upon individual rights but also to drive a wedge between the state and its citizens. This disjunction is felt most acutely by law-abiding individuals who, far from feeling protected, find themselves hindered by regulations that seem to serve little purpose other than curtailing their freedoms. These policies too often impose sweeping restrictions on responsible citizens without targeting the root causes of violence, creating a sense of abandonment and frustration. For those living in rural or economically disadvantaged areas, where police response times can be painfully slow, the state's unwillingness to provide effective protection leaves them feeling forced to choose between self-defence and compliance with laws that appear indifferent to their unique needs and vulnerabilities.

What compounds this sense of isolation is the government's apparent unwillingness to address the very forces driving crime itself. This discrepancy between regulation and reality has fostered a deep scepticism about governmental priorities. The flow of drugs across borders remains largely unchecked; human trafficking networks continue to operate with alarming ease; organised crime flourishes in urban centres. And yet, instead of tackling these fundamental threats, governments appear more focused on imposing restrictions on lawful citizens individuals who seek nothing more than to protect themselves and their families. It is a perplexing and troubling dynamic. One cannot help but wonder: why, amid a climate of escalating criminal activity and porous borders, does the government choose to target its law-abiding populace instead of those who destabilise society?

This bewildering contradiction undermines public trust and frays the fabric of civic responsibility. Law-abiding gun owners are keenly aware of the threats around them, and they understand, perhaps better than most, the vulnerabilities that arise when criminals can act with impunity. However, government actions or inactions seem to suggest a prioritisation of symbolism over substance, where restrictive laws serve to signal governmental action without addressing the root causes of violence. This only serves to widen the gulf between citizens and those who claim to protect them. It is a disheartening reality that, instead of tackling crime at its source, many Western governments have become entangled in a cycle of regulation that often penalises responsible individuals rather than confronting the hard truths of criminal enterprise.

In communities where the ability to rely on state protection is minimal, citizens have historically taken pride in self-sufficiency and responsibility. Yet, with each additional restriction, these communities feel further disenfranchised, their values and needs ignored in favour of policies seemingly designed with urban or politically-driven agendas in mind. Gun control policies that neglect the importance of self-defence in areas with limited police presence disregard the unique circumstances these citizens face. For them, owning a firearm is not merely a right but an essential aspect of personal and communal safety. When government regulations strip them of this means of protection, it sends a clear message: their security is not a priority.

This policy's failure to differentiate between criminality and responsible ownership perpetuates a damaging cycle. Law-abiding gun owners are left to navigate an increasingly complex and restrictive legal landscape while criminals, unbothered by such regulations, continue to acquire weapons through illicit means. Instead of creating safer societies, these restrictions effectively disempower those who follow the law while leaving the criminal underworld largely unaffected. The disparity grows starker with each new regulation aimed at citizens rather than criminals, with each initiative targeting firearms without addressing the factors that drive individuals to crime. It is a glaring oversight, one that suggests a government either blind to the needs of its people or, worse, indifferent to them.

One might rightly ask: what is the purpose of policies that seem so disconnected from their intended outcomes? Why, in a time when organised crime, drug trafficking, and human trafficking operate across borders with shocking ease, does the government focus so intently on controlling the actions of its most responsible citizens? Why are borders left open, criminals left unprosecuted, and traffickers given free rein, yet law-abiding individuals find themselves increasingly persecuted? This approach is not only misguided but counterproductive, undermining the very principles upon which a free and secure society is built.

Such policies betray a dangerous short-sightedness. The emphasis on restrictive laws aimed at citizens who contribute to society stands in stark contrast to the leniency afforded to those who actively seek its destabilisation. If the government is unwilling to address the flow of drugs and firearms across its borders, the rise of trafficking, and the spread of organised crime, then citizens are left to wonder whom the law is designed to protect. Are these measures truly about public safety, or are they simply mechanisms to exert control over a compliant populace while evading the tougher, more complex challenges posed by organised crime?

This divergence between intention and impact is more than just an administrative failing; it represents a deep betrayal of trust. For a government to turn its back on the security concerns of its citizens while allowing criminal activity to go largely unchecked is, at best, a sign of severe mismanagement and, at worst, a deliberate marginalisation of those who believe in the right to self-defence and personal responsibility. The enduring question, therefore, is this: why do governments appear more invested in restraining their law-abiding citizens than in prosecuting those who threaten society's stability? Until this question is addressed, the rift between citizens and the state will continue to grow, with trust eroded and communities left vulnerable, unsupported, and, ultimately, less secure.

A Need for a Balanced, Evidence-Based Approach

This analysis of the failures in current gun control approaches underscores the urgent need for a paradigm shift. It is clear that the current trajectory, driven by restrictive policies that do not reflect modern threats or address criminal realities, is unsustainable. Laws that are difficult to enforce, politically motivated, and disconnected from societal needs will continue to exacerbate the divide between lawful citizens and criminals. As we move forward, there is a clear imperative to reassess gun control approaches and develop policies that are both enforceable and adaptable.

In the following chapter, I will outline specific policy recommendations designed to bridge the gap between intent and reality. These solutions will be grounded in a commitment to evidence-based policy, aiming to protect citizens' rights while addressing the criminal exploitation of firearms – ensuring that future approaches to gun control serve society as a whole rather than fragmenting it further.

Chapter 11: Towards a Balanced Approach: Recommendations for Gun Policy Reform

In this concluding chapter, I aim to propose a nuanced, evidence-based framework for gun policy reform one that recognises the rights of individuals to defend themselves while seeking to mitigate the illicit circulation of firearms among criminal elements. Throughout this book, we have explored the complexities and failings of current policies and the harsh consequences for law-abiding citizens left vulnerable to the whims of well-armed criminals. Here, I shall lay out a series of recommendations that address these issues holistically, balancing the imperatives of public safety and personal freedom.

Strengthening Border Controls and International Cooperation

In addressing the pressing issue of illegal firearms crossing borders, a fundamental step in any gun policy reform is, indeed, the tightening of border controls. I see this as not merely a matter of placing additional personnel or barriers at borders but as a multi-layered strategy encompassing infrastructure upgrades, technological advancements, and a robust framework for international cooperation. A secure border, in this context, means a fortified and intelligently managed checkpoint that's resilient to the ever-evolving methods of weapon smuggling and trafficking.

One can consider the recent commitments from leaders like those in the United States, where now President (Elect) Donald Trump has indicated plans for a strengthened stance on border security, deportations, and controlled immigration policies. Such measures, although politically charged, could have a considerable impact on the volume of illegal firearms crossing into the country. Should the U.S. achieve even a modest reduction in firearms smuggling through these reinforced borders, it could set a precedent for other nations to adopt similar, if less intense, approaches. The deterrent effect alone, paired with the impression that the government is serious about the security and integrity of its borders, could discourage smugglers from attempting the same old routes.

A significant component of bolstering border security involves advanced surveillance technologies. High-definition cameras, automated license plate readers, facial recognition systems, and biometric checkpoints offer border authorities critical tools for detecting illicit activities before they become unmanageable. But even these solutions are not foolproof in isolation; they require support from robust intelligence operations. Real-time data collection, analysis, and sharing with other agencies enable a coordinated response to any detected threats, ensuring that smuggling operations are thwarted before firearms reach urban areas.

Further, a border security strategy must extend beyond physical barriers and into digital ones. Sophisticated data analytics and machine learning systems can scan trade and travel records to identify patterns consistent with smuggling, such as unusually frequent trips by known offenders, suspicious freight imports, or unexplained variations in cargo declared and delivered. This type of predictive approach has been somewhat successful in drug enforcement operations, and it holds immense promise for countering gun trafficking as well.

One of the more compelling strategies that I would advocate is the development of cross-border task forces and intelligence hubs focused specifically on weapon smuggling. Currently, the U.S. and Mexico conduct sporadic joint operations targeting drug and weapon trafficking. However, in many cases, this collaboration is hindered by political friction and limited funding, resulting in intermittent efforts with fluctuating efficacy. By establishing a structured, continuous task force dedicated to intercepting firearms, both countries could benefit from an uninterrupted flow of shared intelligence, standardised communication protocols, and perhaps even integrated databases that allow for real-time tracking of suspects and firearms. Imagine the potential of such a task force operated with the full backing of both governments, equipped with cutting-edge tracking technology and proactive intelligence gathered not only from border checkpoints but from organised crime hotspots across the continent.

In Europe, the need for strengthened cooperation is equally, if not more, critical. Eastern Europe, where military-grade firearms are often sourced due to remnants of the former Soviet Union's stockpiles, is a primary funnel for weapons flowing westward. Criminal groups throughout Western Europe exploit these established routes, moving firearms across the continent with relative ease. Greater European Union integration has meant freer movement across borders; however, it has also enabled traffickers to exploit jurisdictional gaps. A European-led initiative that prioritises cross-border intelligence-sharing agreements and a synchronised approach to monitoring Eastern European arms suppliers could stymie these flows effectively. By developing joint enforcement hubs, the EU can set a standard for collective vigilance, with dedicated teams trained to intercept and dismantle these weapon smuggling operations before they have a chance to reach the streets of major cities.

Additionally, international collaboration on firearm trafficking cannot overlook the importance of policy consistency between nations. Varied laws between countries enable traffickers to exploit legal loopholes. Harmonising firearms legislation among allied countries, especially regarding licensing, firearm component trade, and possession penalties would create a far less attractive environment for trafficking. For example, if the penalties for trafficking firearms were standardised across the U.S., Canada, and Mexico, this unified front could undermine traffickers' strategies of relocating operations to whichever country offers the lightest sentence or weakest enforcement.

Addressing the role of corruption, too, is paramount in securing borders against weapon trafficking. Instances of border officers or officials being bribed to allow contraband through have undermined countless anti-trafficking efforts. This is particularly concerning in regions where organised crime networks have significant financial influence. A long-term commitment to monitoring border officials, including rotating personnel, frequent integrity testing, and incentivising whistleblowing, would address the systemic issue of corruption that so often undermines border control efforts.

Equally vital is the cultural shift necessary within law enforcement agencies on the ground. Many of these organisations operate under outdated paradigms that don't recognise the interconnectedness of modern criminal activities. Given the linkages between human trafficking, drug smuggling, and weapon trafficking, it would be prudent to cultivate a multidisciplinary approach where customs and immigration officers are trained to identify and respond to all forms of organised crime, recognising that, for example, a drug bust might also reveal a firearm trafficking ring.

Finally, there is an opportunity to leverage advances in forensic science to identify and trace trafficked firearms. Systems like the National Integrated Ballistic Information Network (NIBIN) in the U.S. allow law enforcement to link recovered firearms to previous crime scenes, effectively tracing the "life" of a weapon from one crime to the next. Expanding the use of such technologies internationally could provide law enforcement with invaluable data, offering leads on trafficking networks based on ballistic evidence alone.

Ultimately, a secure border is not just about restricting entry but about establishing an ecosystem of vigilance, collaboration, and cutting-edge technology that can anticipate and respond to the complex networks of weapon trafficking that so often evade detection. With leaders like Donald Trump emphasising a fortified approach to border security, there may be a significant shift in how border integrity is approached on a global scale. Should the U.S. see success in implementing stringent border control measures, other countries may well follow suit, recognising the benefits of a well-protected border as both a deterrent to organised crime and a shield for public safety.

In sum, a reformed approach to gun policy that prioritises secure borders is not merely reactive but proactive, pre-emptively blocking criminal activity before it permeates society. This balance protecting the right of citizens to self-defend while ensuring borders are strong and law enforcement empowered is essential in reshaping a gun policy that safeguards freedoms without compromising safety.

Enhanced Funding and Resources for Law Enforcement

In my view, one of the bedrocks of effective gun policy reform is not only the legislation surrounding firearms but also the substantial support given to our local and national law enforcement agencies. Without well-funded, well-equipped, and well-trained police forces, any policy aimed at reducing gun crime is likely to falter. This goes beyond the simplistic debates around defunding or bolstering budgets; it's about recognising that a strategic, properly funded approach to policing is essential to dismantling the networks responsible for illegal firearms trafficking and improving safety in our communities.

A primary step in this direction must be the targeted allocation of funds towards high-crime urban centres, where police forces are often stretched beyond their limits. This includes comprehensive training programmes focused specifically on the challenges posed by illegal firearms. These specialised programmes should equip officers with skills in firearms interdiction, tactical response, and community-focused engagement. The value of training in firearm interdiction, for example, cannot be understated officers trained in recognising trafficking patterns, handling volatile situations, and conducting high-risk interventions are far more effective at intercepting firearms before they can be used in violent crimes. Moreover, in a climate where arms trafficking frequently overlaps with other crimes such as drug trafficking and human smuggling, comprehensive investigative training is vital.

Investment in advanced forensic technology is another indispensable component. Police forces must have access to state-of-the-art ballistics analysis tools and databases that enable them to trace firearms and ammunition used in crimes. Imagine, for instance, a situation where a firearm retrieved from a crime scene can be linked back through forensic technology to its last known legal sale or its previous connections to other crimes. Such information is invaluable in reconstructing the journey of a weapon through various hands, connecting dots that could lead to the dismantling of broader trafficking networks.

In the age of digital transformation, police forces should also be equipped with robust surveillance systems, including drones and secure communication channels. Drones, particularly, can revolutionise the way officers monitor crime-ridden neighbourhoods without placing personnel in harm's way. With the ability to cover vast areas quickly, drones can capture real-time footage of activities and relay it back to police control centres, allowing for immediate responses to incidents or suspicious behaviour. For example, a drone equipped with night-vision technology could help pinpoint the movements of individuals in known trafficking hotspots, or it could be used to safely pursue and monitor fleeing suspects. Paired with secure communication systems, these tools can greatly enhance the speed and effectiveness of police responses, reducing the time it takes for officers to intervene in potentially dangerous situations involving firearms.

Another vital aspect is the enhancement of secure, centralised databases. These databases should be accessible by authorised personnel across various jurisdictions, not only at the local and national levels but ideally with a structure that supports cross-border cooperation where relevant. As firearms trafficking often involves complex international supply chains, particularly with the import of illegal firearms from abroad, the ability to swiftly share information and cross-reference suspects or suppliers in real-time with international law enforcement agencies is crucial. For instance, a firearm smuggled from Eastern Europe and recovered at a British crime scene should immediately trigger a collaborative effort with European law enforcement agencies if data reveals patterns linking it to a broader trafficking operation.

Moreover, any investment in police resources should include a commitment to community-based policing initiatives that foster trust between law enforcement and the public. This is especially important in areas where the public may feel disenfranchised or sceptical of law enforcement due to past experiences. By engaging with the community, police officers are better positioned to gain intelligence from locals, gather tips that might otherwise remain unknown, and address concerns related to gun crime in a way that feels supportive rather than authoritarian. For example, officers who regularly engage with community leaders and conduct outreach programmes can build a rapport that might encourage residents to report illegal firearms activity without fear of reprisal. A community that sees the police as an ally, rather than an enforcer, is more likely to cooperate in efforts to rid their streets of criminal weaponry.

Alongside this, there must be a renewed focus on protecting police officers themselves, whose safety is paramount in carrying out these intensified enforcement duties. Policymakers should consider protective measures for officers engaged in high-risk gun-related operations. Modern protective gear, including bullet-resistant vests and tactical equipment tailored to gun crime interventions, is not a luxury but a necessity for those who put their lives on the line. The physical and psychological toll on officers regularly exposed to gun violence must not be underestimated, and there should be systems in place, such as mental health support, to help them manage the pressures of their work.

It's also essential that the public recognises the complexities and dangers involved in combating gun crime. In too many cases, the perception of law enforcement is reduced to a caricature of policing without an appreciation for the intelligence, collaboration, and nuanced decision-making required to tackle deeply rooted firearms trafficking networks. A strategic approach to public communication such as community meetings or public information campaigns can help clarify the importance of enhanced policing resources in fighting gun crime effectively. Educating the public on the ways that investments in technology, training, and protective equipment empower police to make our streets safer fosters an environment where police efforts are respected and supported.

In conclusion, supporting our police forces means much more than simply increasing budgets. It's about adopting a holistic approach to law enforcement that leverages technology, builds community trust, and provides officers with the resources and training necessary to confront gun crime at its roots. Only then can we hope to dismantle the criminal networks that profit from firearms trafficking, restore a sense of safety to our communities, and ensure that law enforcement can fulfil their duty effectively and safely?

Integrating Modern Data and Technology in Gun Policy Implementation

In today's world, where data-driven insights have transformed countless industries, the approach to gun policy must also evolve to harness these capabilities, moving from reactive, blanket legislation to policies crafted with precision, sensitivity to local contexts, and agility to adapt to emerging threats. Advanced analytics, artificial intelligence, and data mining offer governments a toolkit that has never before existed one capable of transforming the nature of gun policy by predicting, pre-empting, and specifically addressing the root causes of firearm-related violence in different areas.

Firstly, with the rapid expansion of AI-driven predictive analytics, we can identify patterns in gun-related crime at a granular level. By analysing data points from various sources such as crime reports, community demographics, socio-economic indicators, and even social media posts AI algorithms can identify specific areas at heightened risk of illegal firearm activity. Imagine being able to forecast potential hot spots for gun trafficking or gang activity weeks before they flare up; by understanding the factors contributing to risk, resources can be channelled precisely where they are needed most. This approach could help tackle urban violence, where firearms are commonly used by organised crime groups, as opposed to rural areas where illegal firearms are more likely tied to different types of activity.

Another powerful tool in this data-centric approach is social media data mining. Social media platforms contain a wealth of information some of it even public that, when responsibly accessed and analysed, can provide critical insights into criminal networks and firearm trafficking operations. For instance, by utilising keyword tracking and sentiment analysis on social media, law enforcement agencies can detect conversations or coded language related to gun sales or trafficking, allowing them to intercept and investigate suspicious activity before it escalates. AI-based language processing algorithms can identify the language and behaviour patterns of traffickers, helping pinpoint where sales might be taking place and which individuals or networks are involved. This approach is not about infringing on privacy rights but about using already available data to protect communities.

Facial recognition technology, when ethically and responsibly implemented, could also serve as an invaluable tool in the fight against illegal firearms. For instance, facial recognition can assist in tracking known traffickers or individuals previously associated with illegal firearm activity. This is particularly valuable in public spaces like transport hubs, borders, or known trafficking routes where surveillance footage can be cross-referenced with databases of known offenders. Such real-time identification can prevent potential criminal activity before it unfolds while allowing law enforcement to monitor high-risk locations without the need for intrusive physical interventions. However, these technologies must be employed transparently and with strict oversight to prevent misuse or misidentification, particularly given the potential for biases in facial recognition systems.

AI-powered predictive modelling can also play a significant role in identifying communities most at risk for illegal firearm penetration based on social and economic factors. By analysing trends such as income levels, unemployment rates, or educational attainment, governments can deploy targeted social interventions alongside law enforcement efforts. For example, predictive analytics might reveal that certain impoverished urban areas are not only more susceptible to gun crime but also lack adequate youth engagement programmes or educational opportunities, factors known to drive individuals toward gang involvement. A policy that combines increased police presence with social investment in these high-risk areas can tackle both the symptoms and root causes of gun violence, providing a more holistic approach than enforcement alone.

Additionally, technology offers promising advances in gun safety features. Although smart guns are still in development, they hold the potential to revolutionise how firearms are stored and accessed, reducing the risk of unauthorised use, accidental shootings, and theft. With biometric recognition or fingerprint sensors, smart guns could allow only verified individuals to fire the weapon, ensuring that a stolen firearm is rendered unusable in the wrong hands. Such technology could be particularly beneficial in addressing domestic firearm theft and protecting families from tragic accidents involving children who find unsecured weapons. While these innovations require further refinement and robust testing to be reliable in high-stakes scenarios, the potential for smart guns to become a standard in firearm safety is considerable.

Moreover, governments should consider establishing centralised, AI-powered databases that track firearm sales, registration, and usage patterns. By aggregating data from multiple sources, these databases can help authorities monitor trends, identify irregularities, and trace firearms back to their sources more efficiently. For instance, if a particular firearm or batch of firearms appears at multiple crime scenes, AI algorithms could alert law enforcement to potential links between crimes or identify emerging trafficking routes. Integrating these databases with international intelligence-sharing platforms would facilitate cross-border cooperation, helping to intercept illegal firearms before they reach high-risk regions.

However, adopting these advanced tools also requires a regulatory framework that addresses privacy concerns and ensures responsible use. The public needs to have trust in the agencies employing such technologies, which means transparency, accountability, and clear guidelines on data usage are essential. Governments should establish independent oversight bodies to review the implementation of AI, facial recognition, and social media data mining in law enforcement, ensuring that these tools are used fairly and responsibly. Regular audits, public reports, and strict data access protocols can help mitigate concerns about government overreach and safeguard citizens' privacy rights while still allowing law enforcement to benefit from technological advancements.

By adopting a tailored, data-informed approach to gun policy, we can transition from one-size-fits-all solutions to flexible, adaptable policies that consider the unique realities faced by different communities. Rural areas may not require the same level of surveillance and enforcement resources as urban centres plagued by gang violence, and data allows us to allocate resources accordingly. Rather than spreading budgets thinly and ineffectively, governments can focus their efforts on regions that need it most, enhancing both efficiency and public safety.

In conclusion, the integration of AI, data mining, facial recognition, and smart gun technology provides us with an unprecedented opportunity to address gun violence in a more precise, effective, and equitable manner. These tools, when combined with traditional policing and social interventions, offer a path toward gun policy reform that is responsive to real-world conditions, adaptive to emerging threats, and mindful of the rights of law-abiding citizens. The future of gun policy lies in data-driven strategies, where informed decisions replace reactive laws, and where a community's specific needs guide the resources and policies that serve it.

Reforming Legislation to Protect Law-Abiding Citizens

The right to self-defence is a deeply ingrained principle that resonates through history as a core human entitlement, yet modern policies in much of the West seem increasingly to discount this reality, leaving ordinary citizens without the means to defend themselves adequately. While criminal elements often find ways to access firearms or other weapons through illicit channels, the public, bound by restrictive policies, remains vulnerable. This asymmetry where law-abiding individuals feel disarmed and helpless while offenders operate with relative impunity erodes trust in government and its ability to provide security, a situation made worse by rising crime rates in many urban areas and the underfunding of police forces.

One way to redress this imbalance is to ease certain firearm restrictions for responsible, law-abiding citizens, particularly those who live in remote areas where police response times are inherently delayed. In such regions, residents cannot rely on a rapid law enforcement response in an emergency and therefore need additional means to ensure their safety. Here, self-defence is not a theoretical concept but a practical necessity. A carefully designed system of exemptions or special permits could address this, allowing rural and isolated residents the right to access firearms with the assurance that they are still under appropriate oversight.

Rigorous yet accessible licensing programmes are key to achieving this balance, ensuring that firearms do not fall into the wrong hands while making it practical for responsible individuals to obtain them. Such programmes could incorporate enhanced background checks, focusing on any criminal record, history of violence, or mental health red flags. In addition, these programmes could mandate basic firearms safety and handling courses, providing applicants with the necessary training to use their weapons responsibly. This approach would help foster a culture of responsible firearm ownership, ensuring that those who do have access to firearms are well-prepared and well-regulated.

For urban areas, where the need for armed self-defence may be less obvious but is still a pressing concern given the rise in violent crime, governments should also explore reforms. An intermediate category of defence tools such as non-lethal options, including pepper spray or tasers could be offered with minimal licensing restrictions, ensuring that individuals have at least some means of defending themselves if firearms are not feasible or advisable. Such tools provide a deterrent against attackers, especially for vulnerable populations who might otherwise feel at a disadvantage in dangerous situations.

However, self-defence rights must be more than merely access to defensive tools; they must be protected within the legal framework. This means establishing unequivocal, reasonable guidelines around the use of force for self-defence, particularly regarding what constitutes justified defensive action. Many citizens are currently deterred from defending themselves due to the potential for legal consequences, even when their actions were clearly in self-protection. In some jurisdictions, individuals who act to defend their homes or families find themselves under investigation, or even prosecution, due to ambiguities in self-defence laws. Governments should work to clarify and simplify these legal standards, providing peace of mind that, when individuals defend themselves or others, they will not be unjustly penalised.

In addition to clear legal guidelines, it would be beneficial to provide structured support for individuals who have acted in self-defence, including legal aid and counselling services. By ensuring that such individuals have access to legal representation, counselling, and a fair investigation process, governments can demonstrate a commitment to supporting the right to self-defence without encouraging vigilante action or reckless violence. This approach strikes a balance between upholding justice and recognising the complexity of self-defence situations, especially where adrenaline and fear may influence a citizen's actions.

International examples also provide insight into how policies can be crafted to protect self-defence rights while maintaining strict controls over who can access firearms. For instance, countries such as Switzerland and Israel have frameworks that balance access to firearms for those with legitimate security needs against broader restrictions for public safety. In Switzerland, for example, firearm ownership is permitted but heavily regulated, with applicants needing to meet stringent requirements and pass background checks. Similarly, in Israel, firearms are accessible to citizens living in areas at greater security risk, but only after extensive training and verification processes. These systems demonstrate that it is possible to protect public safety while ensuring individuals are not left entirely defenceless.

Finally, a balanced self-defence policy should acknowledge the evolving nature of threats in the modern world, including the rise of gang violence and the unpredictable nature of terrorist attacks. By recognising that personal safety concerns vary widely across communities, governments can design self-defence laws that address different risk profiles. In regions where crime is statistically higher, particularly violent crime, citizens should have options available that respect both their right to safety and the practical constraints on law enforcement.

In sum, an approach to gun policy and self-defence rights that acknowledges the diversity of security needs, considers geographic realities and implements robust oversight can provide a safer, more empowered society. People must feel confident that, in a time of crisis, they have the means to protect themselves and that the law will stand behind them if they act responsibly. By reforming policies to respect this fundamental right, governments can restore a crucial element of trust the assurance that, while protecting the public, they have not overlooked the personal safety of the individual.

The Role of Government: Balancing Safety and Freedom

At its core, the responsibility of government is to protect its citizens from harm while safeguarding their freedoms. Yet, in many instances, it seems that law-abiding individuals are forced to bear the brunt of restrictive policies, while those who break the law often face minimal consequences. This disconnect raises a difficult question: why are responsible citizens cast aside, left to navigate policies that often seem more focused on punishing the law-abiding than deterring the criminal? Why is there so often a skewed balance that favours criminals and casts doubt on ordinary people's right to defend themselves?

When discussing gun control, it is crucial to recognise that no policy alone can address the complex social issues underlying criminal behaviour. Crime is not merely a product of access to weapons; it is often a by-product of societal failings poverty, inequality, limited job prospects, and, in many cases, a weakening of community bonds and values. If we wish to reduce criminality, we must target the root causes, not just the symptoms. Addressing these factors through robust social programmes, economic opportunities, and community investment may, in the long term, be far more effective in preventing violence than blanket restrictions on firearms.

In this broader context, gun control should not be treated as a one-size-fits-all solution but rather as one tool among many to address safety concerns. And it must be wielded with sensitivity, taking into account regional differences and the specific security needs of communities. It's one thing to impose stringent firearm restrictions in low-crime, densely populated areas with short police response times; it is quite another to apply the same restrictions in rural or isolated regions where people may need to defend themselves due to delayed emergency services. A rigid, blanket approach ignores these practical realities and risks making life more difficult and dangerous for those who pose no threat to society.

A government committed to genuine security for all would recognise that inflexible policies serve no one well. This is why flexibility and responsiveness are crucial to any effective policy on public safety and gun control. In many places, restrictive laws from a bygone era continue to be applied to new and vastly different circumstances, leaving communities vulnerable and the public's sense of security compromised. Rather than adhering to outdated principles, officials need to consult regularly with law enforcement, communities, and experts in public safety to continually refine policies based on empirical evidence, rather than ideological stances. There is an undeniable need for public input on these matters; after all, it is the citizens who experience the immediate impact of these laws.

Transparency and accountability are essential components of this process. When governments impose restrictive policies, it is not enough to simply implement them without further comment. Citizens deserve to know the effects of these measures, how they are improving public safety, and how officials are evaluating their outcomes. Far too often, policy changes are announced with great fanfare, yet their effectiveness is not scrutinised, and the public remains in the dark about whether these changes are achieving the intended results. By fostering open discussion and making policy outcomes publicly available, governments could build trust and engage communities more actively in the pursuit of safety.

Moreover, in striving to keep firearms out of the wrong hands, why do we not see more emphasis on deterring those most likely to use weapons illegally? Rather than devising restrictions that bind the law-abiding, governments should focus on penalties that truly discourage criminal behaviour. Habitual offenders, gang members, and individuals caught in illegal possession of firearms should face substantial consequences that effectively deter them from reoffending.

Instead, too many offenders slip through legal loopholes or face lenient sentences, reinforcing a sense of impunity. Meanwhile, law-abiding citizens encounter endless bureaucracy when attempting to secure a firearm for self-defence, creating the unfortunate impression that policy favours criminals over the public.

Additionally, a balanced approach should consider innovative solutions such as community policing initiatives and social outreach programmes that can preemptively address criminal tendencies. Programmes aimed at at-risk youth, job training for those in disadvantaged communities, and mental health services could address some of the root causes driving crime. Investing in these resources provides long-term stability, reducing the likelihood that individuals will turn to crime in the first place. By viewing public safety through this lens, governments would demonstrate a real commitment to prevention rather than a fixation on restriction.

In summary, protecting the public is not just a matter of imposing more laws but of creating a secure and just society where law-abiding citizens feel protected, and criminals are deterred by meaningful consequences. It requires a government that is unafraid to adapt, continually assessing the impact of its policies on real people's lives, and showing respect for citizens' fundamental rights, including the right to self-defence.

A balanced approach to gun policy reform does not aim to solve all societal ills but to create an environment where responsible citizens retain the right to self-defence while criminals find access to firearms increasingly difficult. This approach, grounded in collaboration, evidence, and responsiveness to social realities, can help bridge the divide between public safety and personal freedom. As we move forward, it is incumbent upon lawmakers, law enforcement, and the public alike to uphold this balance, recognising that genuine security is not the suppression of rights but the assurance that everyone can live without fear or harm.

Epilogue: Reflections on the Future of Gun Control and the Rights of the Law-Abiding Citizen

Writing this book has been an intensely personal journey, informed not only by a lifetime of observation but also by my own experiences with firearms ownership. Over the years, I've been licensed to own various types of firearms across the UK, Europe, and Canada, and this has provided me with a unique lens through which to view the evolving landscape of gun control. The journey, however, has been far from simple; in recent decades, I've seen first-hand how ownership has become increasingly burdensome. Stringent regulations have led to the closure of countless gun clubs and firing ranges, and bureaucratic hurdles have turned what was once a straightforward process into an obstacle course of paperwork and waiting periods. Ironically, while restrictions have mounted for law-abiding citizens, gun crime perpetrated by unlicensed criminals has surged, rendering many of these regulations ineffective against the very threat they purport to address.

Reflecting on the contents of this book, I am struck by a single, undeniable conclusion: current gun control measures often fail to strike a balance between ensuring public safety and preserving individual rights. On the surface, it seems logical to assume that limiting gun access would lead to a safer society. Yet, as explored in this work, reality paints a more complex picture. Stringent gun laws often leave law-abiding citizens feeling defenceless and disillusioned with governments that seem more focused on restricting the freedoms of the compliant than addressing the dangers posed by the criminally inclined.

The realisation is disheartening but undeniable: criminals have become emboldened by a system that has gradually eroded the self-defence rights of ordinary citizens. In places where firearm access has been severely restricted, crime has not abated. Rather, it has morphed, with criminals exploiting an environment in which the citizenry is disarmed and unprotected. My experiences in Canada, the UK, and Europe have shown me how these policies play out on the ground. While ownership regulations tighten, the illicit firearms market flourishes, feeding a parallel economy that thrives on the unmet demands of both criminals and those who seek to defend themselves but are denied legal means to do so.

As I conclude this work, I am compelled to consider what the future holds for gun policy reform. Chapter 11 outlines my recommendations for a balanced, evidence-based approach. The key lies in recognising that gun policy is not a one-size-fits-all solution; rather, it requires a nuanced understanding of each nation's unique cultural, social, and legal landscapes. In advocating for reform, I am not calling for an unrestricted proliferation of firearms but for policies grounded in pragmatism and respect for individual rights. This balanced approach entails strong measures against criminal access to firearms while ensuring that responsible citizens retain the means to protect themselves.

One of the primary recommendations I put forward is the necessity of fortified border controls. The ease with which weapons cross into countries with supposedly strict gun laws is an ongoing paradox, highlighting the inadequacy of regulations that fail to consider transnational criminal networks. Only by addressing the root causes of illegal firearm trafficking can we hope to stymie the flow of guns into the hands of criminals. This will require substantial investments in both manpower and technology, as well as an unprecedented level of intelligence sharing across borders. It is a challenge, but one that we must meet if we are to uphold the integrity of our national laws.

Further, I argue that law enforcement must be sufficiently funded and supported to confront the realities of modern criminality. In many cities where gun violence is rampant, police forces are stretched thin, often grappling with the dual pressures of restricted budgets and political scrutiny. A society cannot claim to value public safety while simultaneously undermining the very institutions tasked with ensuring it. An adequately funded and empowered law enforcement apparatus is not merely a deterrent but a vital component of a civilised society that respects the right of its citizens to live without fear.

This book also underscores the need for international cooperation in tackling the black-market networks that enable gun crime to flourish. Firearms trafficking is, by nature, a transnational problem, one that can only be effectively addressed through collaborative efforts. The criminal underworld is adept at adapting to legal loopholes and exploiting disparities in national laws. By working in concert, sharing intelligence, and pooling resources, Western nations can present a unified front against these networks. This collaborative spirit must extend beyond regional alliances, recognising that the threats we face today transcend borders and demand a collective response.

In proposing these measures, I have drawn upon examples from around the world, exploring how countries like Switzerland and Canada have managed to preserve responsible gun ownership rights without sacrificing public safety. These case studies demonstrate that pragmatic, well-considered policies can succeed where blanket restrictions often fail. We would do well to learn from these models, incorporating lessons from both their successes and their shortcomings.

As I pen these final thoughts, I cannot help but feel a certain nostalgia for a time when ownership was a simpler matter, when gun clubs thrived, and responsible citizens could exercise their rights without undue interference. Yet I also recognise that societies evolve, and with that evolution comes a need to address new challenges in thoughtful ways. The task before us is not to return to a past era but to forge a path that respects the rights and safety of all citizens.

Ultimately, gun policy reform is about balance. It is about acknowledging that public safety and personal freedom are not mutually exclusive but intertwined. The role of governments, I believe, is not to impose overbearing restrictions but to empower individuals while protecting society from genuine threats. This delicate balance is what defines a free and fair society. As we move forward, I hope that policymakers will heed the lessons of history, considering not just the letter of the law but its impact on the lives of those it seeks to govern.

In closing, I hope that this book has provided readers with a comprehensive understanding of the complex issues surrounding gun control. The discourse surrounding firearms is fraught with emotion, and understandably so. But as citizens, we must move beyond rhetoric and towards informed, rational policies that respect the rights and address the realities of our modern world. This is the challenge we face, and it is a challenge we must meet if we are to ensure a safer, more just society for future generations.

End

Did you love *Disarmed: The Consequences of Gun Control in the West*? Then you should read *The Empire's Warning: What Rome's Fall Tells Us About the West Today*[1] by John Shenton!

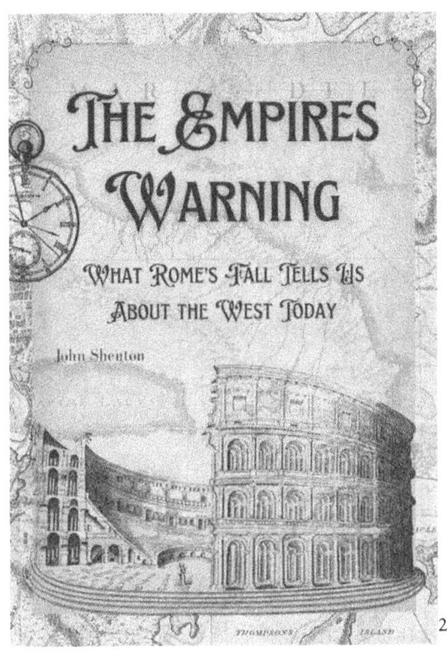

[2]

The Empire's Warning: What Rome's Fall Tells Us About the West Today is a thought-provoking exploration of the parallels between the decline of the Roman Empire and the challenges facing modern Western civilisation. Drawing on extensive historical research and personal experiences—such as walking Hadrian's Wall and visiting Roman Vindolanda—the book examines whether the West, like Rome, is destined to fall or if it can learn from history and avert a similar fate.

The book begins by comparing the Roman Empire at its zenith to the post-World War II West, which, like Rome, has enjoyed

1. https://books2read.com/u/mdaQZ5

2. https://books2read.com/u/mdaQZ5

unparalleled dominance in military, economic, and cultural influence. Yet, just as Rome's decline came in slow, subtle stages, so too do the signs of Western decay. Political instability, economic stagnation, military overreach, and the breakdown of public trust are examined in detail, offering readers a compelling account of the present-day West through the lens of history.

Chapters such as The Role of Governance and Economic Stagnation and the Collapse of Infrastructure delve into the systemic issues that contributed to Rome's downfall, highlighting alarming similarities in Western governance, corruption, and fiscal irresponsibility. Immigration and Integration offers an in-depth analysis of how mass migration destabilised the Roman Empire and draws comparisons to contemporary immigration challenges in the West.

As the book progresses, it asks whether the West can reverse its current trajectory. In Can Decline Be Reversed?, historical lessons from figures like Diocletian and Constantine are explored, along with modern policy recommendations for economic reform, political renewal, and societal cohesion. The final chapter, The Future of Western Civilisation: Decline or Transformation?, poses the question of whether Western society can transform itself in the face of technological disruption, geopolitical shifts, and cultural decay.

Ultimately, The Empire's Warning is a call to action. While the story of Rome is a cautionary tale, the book remains cautiously optimistic, offering insights on how the West might rejuvenate itself through bold reforms and renewed civic duty. In a world of growing uncertainty, this book challenges readers to reflect on the future of their civilisation and the lessons history has to offer.

Also by John Shenton

Business Plan Basics

The Bahamas - More Islands and Recipes Than You Expect!

Collected Musings from Bricks and Mortar to E-commerce

The Smart City Odyssey: Unveiling the Secrets to Traveller-Centric
Software

The Dragon's Gambit: China's Bid for Global Dominance and the
Western Response

Silent Weapon

Business Basics: Money Sources

Influx

Fried Chips

Mandates, Motors, and Misinformation

Echos of Orwell

Control and Chaos

The Empire's Warning: What Rome's Fall Tells Us About the West
Today

Silent Slaves: The Dark Trade of Human Trafficking

Disarmed: The Consequences of Gun Control in the West

About the Author

John Shenton was born in Birmingham, England and grew up in postwar England. He spent several years as a Radio Officer onboard a variety of vessels sailing to the Persian Gulf, the Indian Ocean and South China seas.

With degrees and a background in electronics and computers he has lived and worked within the United Kingdom, Germany, Switzerland and Canada.

While doing so, he established numerous trading relationships in Japan, Korea, the USA, China and other countries.

He has been retired for some time now living in Montréal Canada enjoying golfing, writing, sailing and many other things automotive.

About the Publisher

John Shenton published via Draft2digital

www.ingramcontent.com/pod-product-compliance
Lightning Source LLC
Chambersburg PA
CBHW070516160726

48003CB00004B/1592